After Party

ADVANCE PRAISE

"This is a beautifully honest book of inspiration and transformation that reveals the ultimate truth, when it comes to alcohol there is nothing to "give up" and everything to gain!"

—Andy Ramage,
Best-Selling author of *Let's Do This! How to Use Motivational Psychology to Change Your Habits for Life* and *The 28 Day Alcohol-Free Challenge: Sleep Better, Lose Weight, Boost Energy, Beat Anxiety*

"Drew's story of recovery and overcoming addiction is breathtaking. It's raw, it's real and it's from the heart. Even the darkest times experienced by Drew are written beautifully and he brings you in with him. It's an inspiring read of a ridiculously talented young father coming back from the brink and one which illustrates perfectly that the opposite of addiction is connection. And as Drew reminds you regularly, 'you are not alone'."

—Sharon Hartley,
BBC Radio Presenter/Broadcast Journalist & Co-Host of the alcohol free podcast, *Over The Influence*

AFTER PARTY

Finding the Path to Sobriety

DREW CHARLES

NEW YORK

LONDON • NASHVILLE • MELBOURNE • VANCOUVER

After Party

Finding the Path to Sobriety

Published in New York, New York, by Morgan James Publishing. Morgan James is a trademark of Morgan James, LLC. www.MorganJamesPublishing.com

ISBN 9781631954139 paperback
ISBN 9781631954146 eBook
Library of Congress Control Number: 2020950106

Cover & Interior Design by:
Christopher Kirk
www.GFSstudio.com

Morgan James is a proud partner of Habitat for Humanity Peninsula and Greater Williamsburg. Partners in building since 2006.

Get involved today! Visit
MorganJamesPublishing.com/giving-back

For my family

TABLE OF CONTENTS

ACKNOWLEDGMENTS

Thank you so much to my amazing editors, Cathy and Brett for your assistance in putting this book together. Your encouragement and help has been so crucial to this story's development. Thanks also to Kate Emmerson and Sarah Bullen at The Writing Room. Your support, encouragement and motivation were critical to getting this story together. To my incredible publishers and publishing team at Morgan James I extend my deepest gratitude. I never imagined that this story would see the light of day but your guidance and mentorship has brought my story to life and I am so proud to be part of the team.

To my wonderful wife and daughter, thank you for sticking by me through thick and thin. I could not have achieved much in life without your ongoing support and love. Thanks also to my dear parents, sister, brother in-law and brother. Your help and editorial eyes have made this happen and I couldn't be more grateful. Thanks to Sara Anna, Annie, Sharon and Tricia for your support and encouragement both in sobriety and in encouraging me to write, for reading rough drafts and your constant inspiration. Lastly, to my wonderful sober tribe, you've all been with me every step of the way. I would not have had the courage to get sober or document its progress without every single one of you. Your comments, your stories, your struggles, your advice, it has all helped more than I can express in words. Thank you.

INTRODUCTION

Bright sunshine. The occasional epileptic blasts of solar rays as the sun slips below the skyline, pierces the buildings, blinds me then vanishes. My eyes adjust to the dark, as the sun slips beyond the horizon. Darkness beckons and entices me with false promises. Gripped by something unseen. People are thrust into their illusory cure for the monotony and drudgery of the weekdays. The heady dream of Friday night drinks promises to cure the working week.

Slipping through tables of revelers, through drinking masses, through the smoke filled beer gardens, the occasional pockets of dense fog hiding the bright eyes and flushed cheeks of intoxication. Arriving at a bar of stainless steel and cheap wood veneer. I fish around in my pockets to find my credit card.

xiv | **AFTER PARTY**

I order a beer in eager anticipation. I get handed my drink, my blood quickens, my eyes dilate, receptors fire in excitement, waiting. My heart races as the cool liquid hits my lips, threatening to quench a thirst that is only just now intensifying. Liquid cascades down the back of my throat and my brain's passion to eradicate itself ignites.

I drink deep. Countless beers pass my lips. Countless drinks sting my pocket. Back through smoke: now potent, thick and dense in the muggy night. Upstairs, past faces, legs and arms, conversations that go nowhere, spit, stench…

Swelling starts in my stomach. It circles like a nymph dancing on the sea, rising like the cleansing tide to moisten the dry sand. It extends up through my body, reaching into my head, which pulsates and shudders under the pleasure blast my brain has been receiving. My fear melts away, and I feel my anxiety dissolving into a sea of emotional oblivion. For a fleeting second I see myself and others connected by the ties of history, a sprawling tapestry into which we each weave our little corner, a small imprint in the vastness of time. My head grows with warmth towards myself, towards strangers, friends, lovers long lost, people never met. The processes of nature, the immensity of the universe, all coalesce around me in a momentary, fleeting, pinprick of time in seasick-laden, wobbly euphoria, a tainted type of bitter happiness, a tantalizing taste of something I can never achieve in this state…

But it's all too much. The warmth grows to heat. Swaying descends to spinning. People's eyes bulge, faces contort, it's too hot. I race through crowds, bumping people as I go, descending through smoke, which hits my lungs like knives as the bitterness rises from my stomach. I burst into the bathroom, the stainless steel prison, as the contents of my stomach make a desperate dash for freedom and the night's fleeting perfection comes to its ultimate place of residence: in a dirty toilet with no seat.

Does this ring a bell? This is the story of countless nights that have all ended up more or less the same: drunk and high, feeling terrible and more times than not, making myself physically ill. It's a familiar story and one that we all too often take for granted. For many of us, our relationship with alcohol begins when we are children. Whether it's transmitted to us via our parents, extended families, or peer groups, we begin imbibing alcohol-saturated imagery from day one. We live in a booze-drenched culture. Celebrations, commiserations, stressful situations, boring situations, happy occasions, sad occasions, stressed at work, success at work, marriage, divorce, dates, breakups, out with friends, at home with friends, out alone, at home alone. All these occurrences are a common cause to crack a bottle of your favorite drink and begin the steady path to intoxication.

This is the story of how I got myself into and then out of trouble with booze and drugs. It's the story of a high achieving, high functioning binge drinker, partier, hedonist, and eventual alcoholic. I have always lived life with these separate silos. I have lived as an academic with a PhD, as a musician who did multiple international tours, as an avid sportsman and as a devoted husband and father to a gorgeous girl, all while spiraling into a ball of anxiety, drinking excessively, and taking drugs to the point of near death.

Many, many of us struggle with substance abuse in the shadows. We are ashamed. We feel alone. We feel inadequate. We feel resentful of the fact that we seemingly see everyone around us drinking moderately, drinking without the kinds of dependence, or lack of control that we know we have when we drink, when we smoke, when we do lines off dirty toilet cisterns in the early hours of the morning, when we swallow pills into the daylight hours, with no food, no water, and no sense. You are not alone. There are many of us out there. Many of us hold down good jobs. Many of us are still holding together families, paying the bills, taking our kids to soccer practice, living in clean houses, taking care of everyone else's needs, and neglecting our own. Many of us keep up appearances while at the same time kicking ourselves every time we stumble into bed drunk out of our minds. Many of us saying, "never again," as we mutter pathetically into the toilet, or bucket, after another night or day of failing to moderate our liquor consumption. You are not alone. There are many of us. But there is a way out.

This is the story of how I dug myself out of this spiral of excess. I write this not to preach, but merely to show you how one person discovered that sobriety is not the impossibly boring state of living us heavy drinkers always feared it would be. Far from it. Sobriety has turned out to be filled with joy and excitement in ways I could never have predicted when I was stuck in the loop of drinking and drug taking. This is the honest account of my first year of sobriety, how I did it and more importantly, why I did it. I tell you this in the hope that anyone who battles with alcohol and drugs, or just feels curious about sobriety, can take solace in knowing that life not only exists beyond alcohol, but that it sings with a clarity and depth of emotion I never thought possible.

It was June 2018. I arrived home after a five-week tour of Europe with my band having drunk to the point of passing out or vomiting every single night. This was the culmination of a year and a half where we toured overseas four times. I got home with my relationship in tatters and my finances in ruins. I came home and did everything that I thought I could to repair my marriage and be a decent father after so much time away. But I didn't address my drinking. Instead, I retreated indoors, and while I initially slowed down on the partying, my drinking became more habitual, more chronic and by September, I was getting drunk every night at home.

I was bored in my job. I was embittered about my experience of "chasing my dream." I was rightly resented at home. My anxiety was getting completely out of hand, and it led me to fall back on the only coping strategy I'd ever known: drugs and booze. So back into partying I went. My wife stopped trusting me and my word was useless. Bereft of creativity, bereft of energy, and rapidly losing the will for pretty much anything, I started to think about checking out of life and just drinking myself to death in solitude. I felt like all my choices had just burdened people. I felt like a complete waste of space and I had managed to alienate the people closest to me.

Then one night, I said to my wife I would come straight home after my show that evening. I was driving. I wasn't going to drink. I ended up getting home well after sunrise the next day after doing lines of cocaine and drinking straight gin at a mate's house. I stumbled in, vomited everywhere and begged myself to remember that feeling of utter shame and humiliation. But there was also a feeling of resolve that this life wasn't me. I began to research options for quitting.

I didn't say a word to anyone. For the first time in my life, I just wanted to get sober and stop being that guy who squanders every opportunity and ends up in mid life being a tragic figure. There's a certain romance in the figure of the tragic drunk. But it's an illusion. It's a life with one foot in the grave and the emotional range of a toddler's attention span. It's half a life. I didn't want that. I still don't.

I've learnt some serious lessons along the way, but the biggest one is that not drinking isn't the panacea for life's troubles. It hasn't just fixed everything for me. But it has allowed me to identify a range of things that weren't working and that I wasn't addressing. Booze and drugs were getting in the way of every aspect of my life. I have heaps of stuff to work through, but now I believe I can, and will. Here's how it all unfolded.

CHAPTER 1

After finally getting to the point where I was managing to put away two bottles of red wine a night at home, I finally accepted that drinking had got the better of me. I was increasingly doing the embarrassing march to the local liquor store, where I'd buy wine in the afternoon only to return again later that evening for more supplies. At this point I would almost always buy a two bottle special, and often accompany that with a bottle of the strongest Belgian beer I could find as well just to give me that option to drink myself to sleep.

I also kept a selection of single malt whiskey in the cupboard to make sure I had plenty of options so my wife wouldn't see just how much I was drinking. Keeping many booze varieties on hand so you can take little nips from each was, I thought, a great way to hide my increasing consumption. I don't think I was fooling anyone. I was fooling myself less and less.

One night, when my wife was away for the weekend and I was home alone with my daughter, my solitary drinking finally sparked me into action. I wanted to watch the football and prepared the refrigerator for it. I was telling myself I loved my new quiet life at home after a hectic year of touring overseas with my band. In reality, I was drinking too much to really have any clear conception of what happiness actually looked like. My wife left the house and by the early evening I thought I'd reward myself with a whiskey as I cooked dinner. That was promptly followed by a second. I fed my daughter and got her ready for bed as we watched the pre-game entertainment. I cracked my first beer. I was on my best behavior, so I got her to sleep before half time. I then proceeded to drink the entire six-pack, then a bottle of wine. I then opened a second bottle and through a cloudy alcohol induced stupor I began to reflect on what I was doing. "What if something happens to your child, the most precious thing in your life? You are absolutely wrecked. What possible help can you be?" This negative spiral turned dark, as it so often did, and the thoughts of whether she might be better off without me began circulating as the wine continued to flow, its red luster promising to ease the pain, but delivering, as always, the brutal body blow of more self-loathing, more guilt, more despair.

But I'd begun to see through alcohol's veil and the desire to stop drinking had started to come out of the recesses of my mind. What started as a subtle tapping was becoming a loud knock on the booze-soaked fog of my consciousness. I went to bed.

I awoke, as I so often did, with parched lips, a pounding head, deepening scars on my liver, and an increasing desire to step off this ridiculous treadmill. How do we finally decide? What tips us over the edge? It went something like this…

"I'm leaving now." Muted silence hung heavy in the cool September air.

"I'll see you soon." No response. She'd heard it all before. Empty promises. Empty plans. Empty lives. I kissed her on the forehead, as the cool exterior of her face momentarily cracked letting out a small, almost imperceptible wince at the touch of my lips on her brow. I closed the door as I left.

I stepped out into the quickly darkening night. The cars piling into the city, the bitumen a sea of red glowing eyes peering into the urban streets, ferrying faceless masses into the heart throb, the engine room that houses the city's grimy nightlife. I drove in a fog.

I arrived at the bar. I unloaded my drums and set up in good spirits. It was shaping up to be a busy night. People were already tipping in, hooking their veins up to alcohol's intoxicating sting, the cool long draughts of beer and wine that offer the chance of forgetting the trials of the week. My band mate passed me a beer.

"Just one, mate. Driving tonight."

"Whatever you say, buddy."

I drank it like a man stranded in the desert who had just found water at a hidden oasis. What was supposedly being quenched was suddenly ignited. Flames were fanned as the cool water from my oasis proved to be laden with salt. The thirst…

"I'm going to the bar, anyone need anything?" My band mate asked.

"I shouldn't. It probably tips me over the driving limit," I replied.

"You could probably have one more without too much trouble," He said. He wasn't trying to twist my arm. It was more of a passionless statement of fact. I probably could have one more safely. But would I stop at one? Could I stop at one?

"Yeah, why not. Grab us one, buddy."

"Can do, mate."

I drank the beer. With each sip I felt my resolve weakening. Felt the promises I'd made to my wife obscured in the haze of my increasingly beer-soaked memory. It was now my turn to further destroy my chances of driving home at a sensible hour like I originally planned.

"Who wants another drink?"

Many more drinks passed through our lips. We came off stage and headed to the bar for another round. Then suddenly through the now drunkenness another impulse began to beckon.

"Hey man, do you have any gear on you?" I asked nervously, searching for a stronger drug than alcohol.

"No. Sorry, dude. Give me sec though. I reckon I could find some pretty easily."

I waited anxiously. I didn't really want to be out partying all night. I had said to my wife that I would play, pack up and then come straight home. It was now twenty minutes after the show and all I had achieved was to get more beers and now ask around for drugs. Me keeping my word to my wife was starting to look less and less probable. My mate returned.

"Bingo," he said, with a wry smile.

We entered into the disabled toilets. He poured out two generous lines of cocaine onto his phone.

"I guess I'm not driving home."

We laughed. I was not laughing inside. I snorted the drugs and my insides shut up. Good. Stop trying to ruin my fun. More beers. More lines. Blur.

Somehow we ended up at a friend's place.

"What have you guys got to drink?" I asked.

"I don't know. Let's have a look."

"No beers. No wine. Ooh, we've got gin."

"Any mixers?"

"I seriously doubt it."

"Oh wait, orange juice?"

"Gin and juice. Sounds good to me."

We tipped the entire contents of the gin bottle into three glasses and then topped it up with juice.

"Blergh. That's pretty strong." We all laugh.

"Woah. You're not wrong."

"Oh well, down the hatch then."

The world became suddenly unstable. The seas of my mind became turbulent. At some point I made the decision to leave and managed to get myself a taxi. I have no memory of the ride home. I got home. My mind was a complete fog, a tumultuous storm of wind, rain and ice. I stumbled to the bathroom. I stood swaying over the porcelain counselor. Then the gin performed one of its most efficient functions and expelled the contents of my stomach as I pathetically moaned trembling appeals to the last remnants of my tattered conscience.

I crawled into bed. The sun was up. I was a wraith.

"Mummy, let's wake up daddy..."

"Mummy, daddy stinks..."

"What's wrong with daddy?"

Words I'll never forget...

Utterly wretched, I finally dragged my sorry corpse out of bed. It was midday. My daughter, fresh-faced and beautiful asking what's wrong with me was a kind of tipping point. She was only two at the time and thankfully will not remember this version of me. This tired, tormented, sick with anxiety, over my own stupidity version of me. I know many stories of paths to sobriety have a rock bottom moment, a realization of life as having descended to its lowest conceivable point. I'm not sure I believe in this defining moment. We can always go lower. And anyway, from the outside, I doubt anyone would have even perceived a struggle. For all intents and purposes, I was still high functioning, still working, parenting, and existing without the signs of outward struggle. Internally, however, it was another story.

But I was definitely fed up. I decided to look up Alcoholics Anonymous (AA). It had twelve questions to ask yourself about your drinking. I answered them truthfully for once. I answered yes to ten of the twelve. The website said if you answered yes to five, then you likely have a problem with booze. I didn't really want to hear this. I wasn't ready for the hard line of AA. I wasn't prepared to hear what I suspected was true, that I was an alcoholic and should avoid it forever. I hid AA away from my life. But I was searching for something, some way to change. I didn't want to continue as I had been.

I looked for alternatives. Then, I remembered hearing about One Year No Beer. I searched for it on the Internet. Even though

I wasn't yet prepared to entertain the thought of quitting alcohol, I at least thought that I could do with a break, a chance to reset, a health kick, just something that at least gave me the sense I was trying again. More than anything, I was alarmed that it was taking two bottles of wine to get a buzz. I'd managed up to three-week stints without alcohol in the past. I'd even managed three months without alcohol when I ran a half marathon in 2013. Surely, I could cope with their 28-day challenge? If nothing else, it would reset my tolerance, and I could spend less money. I joined up on the spot. The weekend's accidental debauchery still hung over me like a cloud of dust, fine particulates of shame, guilt, remorse hitting my lungs and making breathing that bit more difficult.

I paid my money. I joined their private Facebook group. I lurked. I didn't really know what to do or say. The desire to drink was all I could think about. I was suffering mixed emotions: I was petrified to give up alcohol, but I simultaneously was beginning to understand how excessive and problematic my drinking had become. I was down. I was grieving. Grieving alcohol. I didn't want to say goodbye. In a perverse way, it's one of my oldest friends. I couldn't yet conceive of a life without it. Why?

CHAPTER 2

'm sure we've all seen people living on the streets. We've all passed them by. Just the other day I walked passed someone tucking into a bottle of rum on a Tuesday morning on the pavement in front of our local shopping center. When I was young I viewed homelessness as a cautionary tale, as a kind of contextual bogeyman of what happens when you let alcohol take over, rather than being a systemic problem of poverty and sometimes impossibly unfair circumstances. The mind of youth perceives things in black and white terms. I knew as a teenager that alcohol had a leading role to play in people's misery. This didn't stop teenage me from slipping a local alcoholic money to buy us beer. The cycle of addiction and exploitation was even then staring me in the face. But I did not have the eyes yet to perceive it. This exploitative act was one of our main sources of getting alcohol in our early teen years. As was raiding my parents' unlocked liquor cabinet. Such was life in 1990s suburban Australia. Every parent in my neighborhood had a liquor cabinet. Every kid in my neighborhood new the contents of their parents' liquor cabinet intimately. By the age of thirteen, I knew which spirits went together, which ones coagulated when mixed and became undrinkable. But most important of all, I knew which drinks were in there for show, or were old presents just collecting dust. I knew what my parents did and didn't drink. I knew what I could steal and get away with.

The first time I got really drunk I was thirteen. In a display of what I can only describe as a completely idiotic attempt at "manliness," an acquaintance challenged me to a drinking competition. This is precisely as stupid as it sounds, and it is still one of the most cringe-worthy moments of my life so far. But as you'll see, there are plenty more.

Boredom. Suburban afternoons for kids entering into their teens can be the height of tedium.

"You guys want to go skate?"

"Nah."

"Have you guys ever got drunk before?" our acquaintance asked.

"Yeah," I lied. I had been given sips of wine but I had never been drunk.

"I drank like a whole six-pack this one time."

"Yeah?" I was intrigued.

"Yeah, I was so wasted. But I've got a really strong stomach," my acquaintance bragged.

"Whatever," I retorted.

"Want to bet?"

"Nah," I lied. I did want to bet. I hesitated.

"You know what? I guarantee I can drink you under the table," I said, not even knowing what this expression really meant. It means you drink until someone falls down. It means you drink until someone is teetering on the brink of poisoning. It means you drink until you pass out, and possibly die. But I didn't know or understand this at the time.

"You're on. I can drink way more than you any day of the week."

"You're on," I said.

"How are we gonna get the booze?" He asked.

"My dad has a liquor cabinet that he hardly touches. I'll go see what I can find."

I ran home. I foraged through the cupboard as quiet as a mouse. There was nothing that looked appealing. I didn't know what was what anyway. Then, I saw it. Up the back of the cabinet was a bottle of cheap whiskey. I'd never seen my dad or mum drink whiskey. It was unopened. I stole it. I ran to the park that our suburban house backed onto. I met the challenger, along with some of my other friends, who had the sense to avoid this doomed stupidity.

"Let's do this," I said.

I took a swig of the fire-laden poison. I coughed and spluttered and my prepubescent body shuddered and quivered with fear at the invasion of this toxic liquid. I couldn't talk. I was choking on fire. My acquaintance grabbed the bottle and chugged, a long uninterrupted stream of straight whiskey went down his gullet without so much as a cough. I grabbed the bottle, determined to prove myself. To prove to my friends, my parents, and to society at large, that I am indeed, a moron. I drank deep of the amber colored fire liquid. After a while, the fire subsided. My taste buds, my brain, my common sense, were all swimming in inebriation. I no longer tasted anything. I felt utterly euphoric. The small boat of my adolescent consciousness was sailing spritely on a warm ocean of intoxication. I drank more. Why wouldn't I? I was feeling great. More would make me feel greater. I took a long chug. So did my acquaintance, now friend, now brother in alcohol-fueled mania. Before we knew it, the bottle was gone. Youth drowned in the false promises of a neatly packaged bottle. Just a bottle. Those beautifully packaged things that innocently sit on shelves in supermarkets that are plastered on the billboards that bombard us from every last remaining pocket of space in our overcrowded cities.

The seas rose, the winds howled. My brain started to sway under the threat of cyclonic dizziness. I stumbled up the hill. I had to get home. I had sea legs. I felt like I had been far from shore my whole life, the earth swayed and I felt all too starkly the movement of our planet as it hurtles around the sun. I staggered into my home and went to the bathroom. How fast does the Earth spin? Could it just slow down? I couldn't take it anymore. I was drowning, consciousness dimming, eyes now untrustworthy, the light of life now perched at the distant end of a vast tunnel of chemical oblivion. I vomited everywhere and blacked out.

I awoke a full day later. My acquaintance had been rushed to hospital where he had his stomach pumped. He was dehydrated, but essentially okay. I had vomited almost unceasingly throughout the night. My parents were beyond angry. I was so ashamed. They'd called the local doctor who had seen all of us for various ailments since we were born. He'd tended to me while I was vomiting naked, barely conscious. I was so embarrassed. I don't remember this, but my mother informed me years later that I'd written him a letter apologizing and thanking him for helping me. Even at this early age, this kind of behavior wasn't what I wanted. I'd learnt a valuable lesson that I would not take heed of for another twenty-four years. But that doesn't mean it wasn't in there, a small imprint of knowledge where I knew alcohol was not going to do me any favors in the end. Unfortunately, I'm a slow learner and this excursion in stupidity has echoed through my life for over two decades.

Alcohol was always around in my house growing up. My parents were not big drinkers by any stretch of the imagination. In fact, I don't think my mother has ever been drunk. It was more of a social norm. A bottle of wine was on the dinner table each night. It was only ever the one though. From an early age I was allowed a taste. I had a small amount of wine with some water in it, then just the wine. It was all very civilized and would hopefully lead to an appreciation of alcohol that would steer me clear of the inevitable pitfalls of binge drinking. I think my parents did the absolute best they could, and they instilled in me so much that I appreciate about my own personality. But children take their cues less from their parents and more from their peers.

I had such a tightknit group of friends living in our suburban street. There was space. There was parkland to get lost in. There were places to hide, nooks to explore, danger to court. As a father of a four year old now, I cringe at the thought of what

I got up to as a child. There was just a never-ending process of boundary pushing and one-upmanship amongst my friends. This had extremely positive applications when we played sport together and skateboarded together. But it inevitably found its way to more nefarious expressions.

As kids, we ended up discovering alcohol by a process of elimination. First, we tried smoking tobacco. My dad had some old pipe tobacco lying around. Once I became aware of smoking, I desperately wanted to try it. Who knows why? It just looked cool, fun, and something I wasn't allowed to do. This only increased its appeal. We'd be in the park skating, and a small group of us would trawl for half smoked cigarettes and butts that we could squeeze a few drags out of. This became a regular after school past time. I shudder to think at the supreme grossness of this activity. But we wanted to be cool. We wanted to be bad.

When I discovered tins of pipe tobacco in the study, I decided to finally steal one and attempt to roll our own cigarettes. This proved to be one of the most comically doomed efforts of my tiny adolescent life. We tried to roll cigarettes using what must have been the stalest tobacco in existence. My dad hadn't smoked for over two decades. Who knows how old this stuff was? Even more ludicrous was that we tried to roll the cigarettes using toilet paper. Plumes of toilet paper smoke poured into our lungs while stale, old, lukewarm tobacco hit the forest floor of the parkland that concealed our delinquency.

But being young and entrepreneurial of spirit, we tried again. This time we used Post-it notes. This was less doomed, and we were able to extract some of the precious, vile tasting tobacco. It hit my throat like knives, exploding into my lungs and causing me to convulse in fits of coughing, my young asthmatic lungs buckling under the intrusion of this relic from another world. I felt sick. I wasn't sure smoking tobacco was for me. I decided to end my fascination with tobacco. It turns out it just made me feel like utter rubbish. No high. No enjoyment. Just sick. Oh well. On I went with my idyllic childhood. I played sport. I skated. I did the absolute barest amount of homework possible so as not to get held back a grade. Life was good.

As we skateboarded more and became better at it, we branched outside of our suburban enclave into the city skating hotspots. We were around older kids, smoking bongs, drinking cask wine and skating like utter lunatics. I was so intimidated. I was more interested in skating on my own terms in my own area. I retreated. I think that beneath a sometimes maniacal party animal there has always existed a profoundly sensible and some what risk averse human. I don't know when I stopped listening to this sensible voice, but it's always been there, and it would eventually come to the fore when I decided to finally end my relationship with alcohol. But mates of mine loved the thrill of the city. It was only a matter of time before our failed attempts to smoke cigarettes turned to more enticing promises.

I was twelve when I first smoked pot. A friend of mine who was a bit older managed to buy some from the dudes in the city. They also explained how to make a bong, which was the only way to smoke pot, apparently. It would be years before I learnt that you can just roll it up and smoke it like a cigarette and not blast your brain into a million pieces under the shotgun explosion of a bong.

After buying weed, sacrificing a meter of good garden hose and a bottle of Spring Valley orange juice to construct what was colloquially known as a "springer," we waited patiently for a night when one of our parents went out so we could get high. We went into my friend's back yard, packed the ludicrously large cone, and smoked straight pot. I coughed and coughed. I've never coughed so hard in my entire life. That whole night was a complete blur of hilarity. I laughed so hard I was genuinely fearful of tearing my stomach muscles. We walked to the supermarket and did all the stoner clichés.

"Hey man, what are you going to buy?"

"I don't know man. I'm so hungry."

"Have ever tried that fake crab meat they have at the delicatessen?"

"No. Good?"

"Man, it's so good. Let's get some."

"And chips. And instant noodles. And chocolate." I started giggling.

I arrived at the checkout and loaded the veritable haul of junk food. I tried really hard to act straight. I started laughing.

"Um, that's twenty dollars and thirty-five cents." The cashier said looking slightly unimpressed.

"Um, cool. I've only got change, sorry," I spluttered amidst giggles.

I dumped twenty-five dollars on the cash register in small change. The cashier rolled her eyes at us. I lost it. I began laughing so hard, while I tried to help count the spare change.

"You know what? I can't be bothered with this. I take your word for it," she spat out at me.

"I'm so sorry, seriously, sorry…" I was now laughing so hard; I took my bag and we left to gorge on our prized haul.

Now this was fun. Weed was where it was at. But where to get it? We were kids. We had no idea. That was when we stumbled upon the plants drying under the deck of one of our friends' houses. We took our opportunity and grabbed a massive haul of weed. Thus began a year of smoking bongs in the park every day after school. My entire grade six year was awash in bong haze. I would come home from school, go get completely ripped and then come home and eat huge bowls of cereal, then sit down to dinner with my family. I don't know how we got away with it. I nearly didn't.

I had stupidly mentioned some of my covert activities to a kid at school, who promptly told his parents, which was absolutely the right thing to do. I was so mad at him at the time, but in retrospect, he was a decent kid, and a twelve-year-old smoking weed is deeply concerning. I was the one doing the wrong thing, not him for ragging on me. The principal called me into his office and grilled me about it. Still to this day I have never told a more convincing and well crafted on the spot lie.

It went like this:

"Drew, what do you know about marijuana?" asked the school principal.

"Nothing," I replied, flushing red at the embarrassment and nervous dread at being discovered as a drug user at such a young age.

"The reason I ask is that we've heard reports from someone in your class that you've been smoking marijuana."

"I would never do that. I don't even know how. I don't know the first thing about it." This appeal to his better judgment almost certainly worked in my favor. I mean, what kid that age knows about drugs, let alone how to get some or what to do with it once drugs were acquired?

"Well, I've had a concerned parent ring and tell me that you have been doing just that."

"Who called?" I asked in a rare moment of bravado.

He answered. How am I going to get out of this?

But lies spin easily in the minds of youth, particularly youth in the headlights of expulsion. They slip off the tongue with a sincerity that I now look back on and cringe at the ease with which I allowed my moral compass to waver.

I continued by saying, "I think I know what's happened. There's been a misunderstanding. I told him that I *found* some marijuana in the parkland behind my house. We didn't do anything with it. We told the police."

"Did you tell your parents?" He inquisitively prodded.

"Kind of. We weren't really sure what to do. We were a bit scared that we might get in trouble," I said in the meekest voice I could muster.

"I was with my friends who live in my street and we were all playing in the park, as we always do. I found these plants that looked strange and like they were being deliberately grown. My older friend said that they're probably marijuana trees. I had no idea. So we went and spoke to his mother who called the police and they said they'd handle it."

"Okay then. Thanks for telling me what really happened," he answered.

I held it together until I left his office, my legs shaking, my hands trembling. I had gotten away with this purely because of my age. No one really thought a pudgy pre-pubescent kid was actually smoking drugs. But I was.

I don't really know if it permanently affected me. It's really hard to tell. I was so young. I can't imagine it not having some effect on a growing brain. But as with many things in my life, I got sick of it and just stopped. I haven't really smoked pot since. For some reason, it just became tedious and I no longer got anything out of it. It wasn't fits of sidesplitting laughter anymore. Within a few short months it had gone from the absolute height of hilarity, to being just normal, boring, a mundane habit. I put my bongs in the park behind me and focused on sport.

Pot isn't the only thing a kid can get high on. Enter alcohol. After my relatively brief stint as a pothead, I realized that alcohol was more my style. It was also far easier to get. How on Earth did a thirteen year old get their hands on booze? It was easier than you might think. There were a few easy avenues, most of which required some courage and some determination. First and most easy: steal booze from your parents, piece of cake. Just steal grog. This was more of a challenge for me than for some. The drunker the parents, the easier to steal. My parents were never drunk, and I knew better than to get into my dad's wine stash. Even an idiot teenager knows better than to mess with a connoisseur's collection. But there were parties. Parties where the cheap booze was over-catered, refrigerators and pantry cupboards housing cheap wine that would never be missed. Each weekend, these soon-to-be forgotten hoards of alcohol no one would ever miss became our path to quick, easy fun.

The other alternative to procuring alcohol when underage is to ask someone on the street to buy you booze. This was a pain and required patience and zero shame. Looking back, I can't believe that we did this. Even more unbelievable was the success rate of this tactic. Maybe it was just a different time, but this never failed to work. Sometimes, we had to bribe the local homeless bloke. Sometimes, a recently legal eighteen-year-old thought we had serious guts and would help us out. Sometimes, it was just some guy that thought we were funny and threw us a bone. Whatever their reasons, we'd be able to source a case of beer without too much problem. The car park behind the bottle shop would see us exchange our pocket money for the cheapest beer available. We'd then have to conceal the slab inside a jacket, then place it on our skateboard and push the booty back home, to the local park, to the local Grade school, crack beers, skate, fall, laugh, lose ourselves in the euphoria of toxicity intermingling with young, supple brains.

Alcohol's pleasant rush was like slipping into warm comfy clothes. My awkwardness, my insecurities, my anxieties about my weight, my appearance, my skating abilities, all washed away in this thick ethanol smog, this glowing pink haze where I could suddenly talk to girls, I could crack jokes, I could exude charisma, I could let the person I thought I was beneath the ever-growing layers of teenage insecurities man the steering wheel. I was free to be me unencumbered. I didn't know about anxiety, about addiction, about neural pathways, about habitual, ritualistic brain bludgeoning. I was purely a pleasure seeker. A simple hedonist enjoying the anxiety free days and nights.

Looking back on this, I had no malice, no real desire to be bad or to live outside the law, rebel or make waves. I wasn't drinking because of any trauma or problems with my home life.

Far from it. Home was fantastic. I couldn't have asked for a better upbringing, or a better family. My parents, my sister, and my brother, I loved (and still love) them all more than anything. But I loved getting drunk. I loved escaping whatever perceived shackles we have in the throes of youth. If anything, my attraction to drugs and alcohol was more about switching off the internal chatter, about quieting the constant stream of negativity I felt towards myself, my body, my inexperience, my inability to determine life on my own terms, the ultimate irony of youth being that it's through our desire to show how mature we can be that we prove how fundamentally immature we really are.

This was not a bad time of life. In fact, I've always viewed many of these early experiences with alcohol fondly. First kisses, first parties, so many enjoyable adolescent experiences were committed under the protective wing of alcohol's dulling and yet fortifying presence. It's only now with the clarity of sobriety that I look back and think how insane it all was. But I look at the way alcohol exists in our society and can't help but feel that that is equally insane. I was not out of the ordinary by any stretch. I was a typical kid with a typical and socially acceptable penchant for hitting the parties with a decent amount of intoxication to spur me on into the night. This was just growing up in the 1990s in Australia, and I'm sure that many people all over the world would have had remarkably similar experiences.

Nights would begin by some kind of lie to our parents. We'd be staying at someone's house whose parents were either relaxed enough to not care what we did, or who were out. We would procure alcohol using the methods I've mentioned. I stole the cheaper champagne, which was a leftover from my dad's and then my mum's fiftieth birthday parties. We would then travel to a party or a park and commence our simulation of what we thought it meant to party. Drink. Talk trash. Try and meet girls. Try and pick up said girls. Rarely pick up said girls. Okay, never pick up said girls. Go home drunk and even less sure of everything than I was earlier. I would repeat this cycle for many years.

CHAPTER 3

September 2018. So there I was. Wanting to quit alcohol, or at least give it a break. After I signed up to One Year No Beer, I began reading the many Facebook posts about people's struggles with alcohol. I quickly saw that I was not alone. What also struck me was the wide cross section of society that seemed to have problems with drinking. There were nurses, academics, lawyers, personal trainers, teachers, people running their own businesses, people high up in the corporate world, and people struggling financially. They were wives, husbands, mothers, fathers, single people, young people and older people. Alcohol cuts across all parts of our societies, and given how pervasive it is, there are bound to be many, many of us who struggle in silence. Despite taking enormous inspiration from these wonderful people who bravely shared their stories, their trials, their successes and failures, I caved. I drank. One small glass of wine became the whole bottle, despite my best intentions. That bottle became the familiar march to the liquor store at the end of the street. Again.

I reset my sober clock back to zero. I tried again. I wanted to at least be able to say I tried. I lasted five days this time. It was my daughter's second birthday party. I bought myself alcohol free beers and drank about six of them throughout the day. I had them in the basin on ice, along with some full-strength beers.

"What on earth are you drinking there, mate?"

"It's an alcohol-free beer," I replied, a tinge of defensiveness creeping in to my voice.

"Alcohol free beer? You're kidding. What's the point?"

"I don't know mate. I'm trying not to drink booze at the moment. So, I guess, I didn't want to miss out." My cheeks flushed.

"Beer without the booze. Sounds pretty grim to me," he responded in a fairly judgmental tone.

"Try it. It's actually pretty nice." I wasn't sure it was nice. But I was trying desperately hard to not drink alcohol. He took a sip.

"Um, yeah, nah. That's no good. How can you drink that stuff?"

"I don't know. Tastes like beer to me," I replied. "Maybe beer is kind of gross?" I said defiantly.

With some willpower and some determination, I managed to white knuckle my way through this first major social engagement. I made it through an entire day of celebrations, only to reward myself with a wine at its conclusion. I sat down as the remaining guests left. My wife put my daughter to bed, as all the sugar in her system finally ran out and she fell in an adorable heap.

The voice inside whispered, "Go on. Everyone has left. You did a great job today. But you've earned a wine. No one will see. No one will know. Go on." I poured a small glass of red wine. I drank it in two sips. "Go on. You can have another one. Think how many you would have normally drunk today? You're ahead. Everyone has gone. It's fine. Go on. You deserve it." I poured another glass. This one was bigger. I drank it quickly. Too quickly. The voice only grew at this point. "Go on. You were a great dad today. You looked after your daughter. But she's asleep now. You need some reward. You need some you time. Go on." I poured a much larger glass and by the time I'd emptied it, I was tipsy. By the time I was tipsy, my mind was no longer capable of making good decisions. Again. One small glass turned into an entire bottle. This turned into two. Two turned into whiskey, into beers, until I stumbled into bed at 2am completely annihilated. Again. What was the occasion? Getting through my daughter's second birthday without drinking. That is a pretty flimsy excuse for getting drunk. I was running out of excuses, running out of occasions to drink. I started to accept that I was drinking because it was a day of the week. Any day would do.

I dusted myself off again. I recommitted. I reset. I did ten days. Same thing. What was wrong with me? I began reading. I had to educate myself. I had to stop feeling like I was missing out. I needed to change my perception of alcohol. These early attempts were marked by the feeling I was constantly depriving myself, that alcohol was something beautiful, magical, something I wasn't allowing myself to enjoy because of some recently formed puritanical nonsense. I was never going to get sober if I kept alcohol on its pedestal. I read books about giving up alcohol, commonly referred to as "quit-lit." Annie Grace's "This Naked Mind" and Catherine Grey's "The Unexpected Joy of Being Sober" were absolutely essential to shifting my perception of alcohol. I immersed myself in the sober world. I tried to open my mind and understand what drove people to *not* drink. More than that, I needed to understand why people decide they don't *want* to drink. Not in the sense of "I shouldn't drink," but the real change I craved, the elusive mentality of "I don't want to drink." This was the first step to uncovering deeper, more frightening truths that emerged later on in my sober experience, and which we will get to in good time.

These books that I mentioned really helped. But others I read didn't. Some I read and I felt preached at. My inner cynic didn't want to hear about sobriety still. I couldn't really accept that these people were having fun. I even heard their war stories and thought those horrific thoughts of an alcoholic: "I'd like to get drunk with these people before they got sober." I'm not proud of those thoughts. Luckily, we aren't our thoughts. Even the books that didn't resonate with me still introduced the important idea that maybe alcohol is a giant illusion. I heard the messages. But they weren't truth to me. Yet.

Those first few weeks of sobriety were a blur. I had just started a new job. A new job in an organization that didn't really understand itself. This ironically, was a perfect fit for me, as I was still very much struggling to understand myself. On my first day, the manager took us all to a fancy restaurant for lunch. We sat down and the waiter took our drink orders:

"What would you like to drink?" The waiter asked my boss.

"Well, I thought I'd have a cheeky wine." Everyone laughed. I laughed. But I winced. My heartbeat quickened.

"And for you?" He asked my colleague.

"If the boss if having wine, I will too." Again. Laughter. Again, a sharp stab of pained longing.

"And for you, sir?"

"I'll have sparkling water thanks." Good decision. I put the alcohol out of my mind. The last thing these people needed to see was my drinking habits in my first week on the job. I sat through lunch, smiling fake smiles, telling the highly abbreviated truth of my life, revealing the tiniest shred of my professional existence in that forced and awkward way we interact with new colleagues. It was painful. But I got through it. I got through an intensely uncomfortable scenario without resorting to my old crutch.

But it was week one of a new job and it was week one of a newly found interest in sobriety. I was still going to stumble. I was still full of excitement at this job. I had high hopes. It was a great job working in education research. It was in areas I had expertise on subjects I truly care about. It turned out to be basically admin, and I got very bored incredibly quickly. But during my first week, my ugly addict came out of hibernation in a massive way.

My friend and I had tickets to see Johann Hari's lecture at the Melbourne town hall. It was a Thursday evening. Hari is a huge advocate for ending the war on drugs. He is an inspirational author and fantastic public speaker. I had read his books and was extremely excited to hear what he had to say in person.

The night proceeded like this: I arrived at a bar over the road to meet my friend before the talk started. I was a few hours early. I ordered a beer. The awkwardness of being at a trendy city bar alone began heating my cheeks as my darting eyes greedily eyed off the drink on my table. I drank it in three large swigs, nervous energy spurring me on to try and alleviate my discomfort with numbing alcohol. My friend arrived. We got more drinks. We had four more. We realized we were a bit drunk, but we wanted to see Hari speak. We took two tablets of Dexamphetamine each to complement our five schooners of beer on an empty stomach. We sat and watched an amazing talk on addiction and the war on drugs through a moderate amphetamine and alcohol haze. The irony of this was not lost on either of us.

The talk finished.

"Well, that was absolutely incredible."

"Wasn't it? I was so impressed. The man has got so many good points."

"Fancy another beer somewhere?"

"Yeah, just one. I've got work tomorrow."

"Yeah, me too."

We decided to head to a trendy outdoor club. It was Thursday night, but it was going off. We got a large beer each and started knocking them back. We met a young woman who was out on the tear. She was charging. She offered us a bump of cocaine. I had just enough booze and amphetamines in my system to think this was a good idea. Three of us entered a cubicle in the bathrooms and we all snorted a line from my phone. When did I become so seamlessly adroit at sniffing drugs off a phone in the toilets? We headed back to the bar. More beers.

We talked rubbish. I can't recall any massively meaningful utterances but we were having fun and enjoying each other's company. We had a dance. We drank more. But the night wore on and we both had work the next day. The bar shut and I decided I must go home, first week of a new job and all. As I hopped on the train, I realized I was very drunk. The Dexies and the coke had given me the chemical shot that translated into speed drinking. I'd consumed six large bottles of beer on top of the schooners I'd had before the talk, all on an empty stomach with no food to blunt the alcohol's charge to my brain. The train ride was wonky. Why couldn't the driver drive more smoothly? I thought to myself, the alcohol-fueled righteous indignation burning a hole in my insides. Seriously? The train driver? Not the beers and drugs you've consumed? I stumbled home. I was ill. Everything is everyone else's fault, I thought to myself as I emptied the contents of my stomach into the porcelain, the grim retainer of all my darkest dread and near silent murmurings of self-loathing.

All the next day I was cursing my wretched existence, trying incredibly hard not to vomit at work. I took a Valium to calm down. It, combined with the punishment of the alcohol and drugs on my empty stomach, did no favors to my trembling stomach.

"Are you feeling okay? You look a little pale." The genuine concern from my colleague was very endearing.

"I'm okay. I think I might be coming down with something." What a lie. I knew what was wrong.

"Okay, well yell out if you need to go home. It's really quite okay."

"Thank you. I'm sure I'll be fine. I'd like to get that document finished for you before we leave today," I replied.

"But it's really no stress if you're not feeling well."

"Thank you."

It was the first week, I couldn't go home sick because of a hangover. That would be admitting defeat. It felt like such an admission of guilt. Instead, I sat in the work cubicle for half an hour trying not to explode. It was my first week at a new job and I was in this state. I was appalled at myself. But it definitely wasn't my fault...

I couldn't believe I was here. I wanted to die. I promised I'd never ever do anything this stupid again... But the end of the workday rolled around. I bought two bottles of red on the way home... it was Friday night and I drank until I passed out...

I was back to day one. I couldn't keep doing this. That episode really threw me. It was not how I wanted to be living life. I was poisoning myself. A healthy, thirty-six-year-old man should not have to hold back vomit all day at work. He should not have to visit the bathroom six times in a work day because his stomach was in knots from recklessly abusing alcohol, from topping up that abuse with drugs, from trying to alleviate his extreme anxiety by topping that already poisonous cocktail with more prescription drugs.

I was so ashamed. So ashamed and defeated that I again turned to wine. I woke up that Saturday morning feeling once again that my life was slipping away through my fingers. I sat in a pool of anxiety and poison soaked sweat. I saw my life unfold on its current trajectory. I saw my liver, after each night like these, taking more and more punishment, little razor cuts leaving deep scars from which it could never recover. I saw the doctors. I saw the hospital visits. I saw the fluorescent lights that would line my march to cold death. I saw my daughter in her youth losing her father too early. I saw the devastation on her face as she pleadingly looked at me with the contempt and sorrow of someone who knows that their father is too stupid, too weak, too wrapped up in his own problems to put her first and be there for her. I saw the pain on my wife's face as I left her to deal with life on her own, to parent on her own, to do everything we swore we'd do together, alone. I couldn't live with this image. It burned a hole in my consciousness. This is the image that fueled my fire. This got me out of my spiral. When I feel weak. When I want to cave. When I feel I have control and I have cured myself. When I am feeling petulant, cocky, complacent, or depressed, and start chattering about how I have earned a drink, deserve a drink, want a drink, I close my eyes and this image washes away those thoughts.

A year earlier, I had seen a psychiatrist to deal with my increasing anxiety. He put me on antidepressants, which helped a lot initially. But after a while, the anxiety level rose, as did my alcohol consumption. So, a year after I'd first been prescribed medication, I went back to my psychiatrist to get more help. He said, "You need to quit drinking." Yes, I did. But how? He didn't say. He left me on my antidepressants. He then referred me to a psychologist. I knew the shrink was right. But it didn't help. It didn't give me tools or hope, or anything other than a directive. The petulant child in me was resentful at being told what to do, even though I knew he was right. So I spoke to the psychologist. It was much more helpful.

"So, I know you've been suffering anxiety lately. What's been going on?"

"I recently came home from a really big tour with my band," I replied.

"That must have been quite a big change."

"Yeah, it really is. We've had a big eighteen months. We've done several tours. We recorded an album in America too. I don't know. It feels like we have done so much. But it feels like there's nothing to show for it," I said.

"How has it been settling back into life here?" she asked.

"It's been okay, I guess. I'm so glad to be home with my daughter. I missed her so much. It's been harder with my wife. I feel like I pushed her a bit too hard. I spent a lot of time away. It's a big ask with a small child."

"Do you think you've broken something?" she asked.

"I worry I have."

"Can you elaborate on that?"

"I worry that I got so caught up with everything I was doing and trying to achieve that I might have just pushed the relationship too far."

"Do you want to salvage your marriage?"

"Of course. I absolutely do."

"That's good. That's important," she replied.

"I didn't do all this stuff because I was trying to run away or escape. I guess I just chased something I thought I wanted. I got tunnel vision. I know that now."

"Well, we all do at times. The good thing is you can see how that might have affected her now."

"Yeah. I do want to make it up to her. And to my daughter. I feel bad I was absent for that time. I'm struggling to get out of the tour routine and into the home routine."

"What was your tour routine?" she asked.

"I don't know. Get up. Drive. Set up. Drink. Play. Drink. Party all night. Do the exact same thing over and over."

"So your drinking got out of hand?"

"Yeah. It really did. I'm finding it hard to recalibrate my consumption now I'm home."

"How much are you drinking?"

'Too much. I know it's too much," I said truthfully.

"Well, I think you better have a break from it. Don't you?"

"Yeah. I really want to. I just don't know how. Every time I try, I just fail. Then I feel bad that I'm a failure and I drink even more."

"I can give you some resources. Have you looked into anything?"

"Yeah. I signed up with an online support group. Do you think that's a good idea?"

"Absolutely. That's a great first step," she said.

I was glad to hear this. It helped me feel like I'd already begun on the road out of this mess. She walked me through a guided meditation to practice to try and help the anxiety. She also gave me some tips to try and short-circuit the cravings for alcohol.

"When you get hit by cravings, I want you to try and do something to step out of your own mind. I want you to practice observing your own thoughts. Don't judge them. Just observe them. What are they saying? It is a good way to take some of the emotion out of them and start to view them for what they are: just thoughts. Even write them down so you can see them clearly. Can you do that?"

"Yes. Absolutely. Thank you."

I left feeling much more positive about how to tackle this. The same old cycle of wanting to stay sober in the morning and then caving by the evening was not going to work. I had to completely change things, at least for a time. I white-knuckled through my first few weeks sober. I cancelled plans on pretty much everyone. I accepted my vulnerability. I had moments when I felt like I could re-enter the world. But I was struggling, day-to-day, and hour-to-hour. Not many moments went by when I didn't have to grapple with the compulsion to get booze, get drugs and get wasted. I just wanted to get out of my increasingly annoying mind. These first two weeks were marked by shaking, panic attacks, sweats, poor sleep, and chastising myself for being weak and idiotic, a moron who's only accomplishment in life was to somehow manage to tie himself in knots. The self-talk was horrendous. I loathed my friends who seemed able to function and still be themselves while they frivolously carried on drinking. I wasn't yet at the point where I could pursue sobriety as an end in itself. It was still something I was doing for others, for necessity, for doctors, for psychiatrists, for my family. It wasn't for me yet.

But I held out. I did everything in my power to not drink. When I had a drink in hand one night, when I'd finally cracked, I thought of my emerging friends on the One Year No Beer Facebook group. I thought about their struggles, about all those beautiful people who have actually been through real problems, not these upper middle class problems of my own volition. I thought about those real, raw, desperate, successful, inspirational people, and I tipped the beers down the sink. I won little battles like this because of the strength I drew from others who I knew understood. But I also drew immense power from my family. Each time I didn't drink, it was another victory, another day further from the center of a widening spiral, the arms of galaxies careering around supermassive black holes that pull everything towards their irresistible core. Each little victory was a little piece of myself recovered, a little moment of honoring myself, and my family. Each little challenge was a shard of resilience recovered from the brink.

CHAPTER 4

Alcohol was so pervasive during my adolescence that it had intertwined itself deeply into some of life's great rites of passage. At fourteen, I met the first love of my life. It's such a curious age. You feel the intensity of burning hot emotion, but the ability to express it, communicate it and translate it into actions is as clumsy and fledgling in its development as our awkward bodies. I was not a confident teenager in the slightest. I was late to develop physically and I was kind of short and round. This never bothered me much before puberty. I was so confident. I was quick witted and talkative. But by fourteen, the burden of insecurities was starting to mount.

I'll never forget the first night I hung out with her. I had managed to steal two bottles of cheap champagne that were sitting in the old booze fridge in the back room, unmanned and unchecked. I managed to grab one and conceal it in the leg of my jeans using some gaffer tape. It was the 1990s, and baggy jeans were a thing. That made this mode of alcohol concealment ideal.

"Do you reckon we can grab two?" my mate asked.

"Risky. Yeah, stuff it. Let's grab two. I'll grab one and you grab the other one," I said.

"How should we get it out past your folks?"

"I reckon we'll have to use the gaffer tape to the leg trick."

"I hate that. Getting the tape off rips my leg hairs out."

"Oh poor you," I said in the most patronizing tone I could muster. "Do you want enough grog to go round or not?"

"Fair call, wise guy."

I grinned.

I grabbed one bottle. My mate grabbed the other. We quickly taped the cold bottles to our legs and snuck past my parents.

"Where are you heading?" My mum asked.

"We're going to a mate's house," I replied, as the freezing cold bottle was uncomfortably pressing against my lower leg. I tried not to look as uncomfortable as I was.

"Whose house?"

"It's a friend of mine," my mate chimed in. "I met her at work."

"Oh, you've got a job now? Good on you," my mum said in her usual, kind fashion.

"I won't be late. See you later."

"Home before midnight, please," my mum called after us as we bolted to freedom.

We headed to our new friend's house. I walked in and saw her. Time stood still. The faint pant of my shallow breath leaked out of my mouth as her shining eyes reflected the distant starlight from which they were created. Her brown hair, luminescent, radiantly framed the lines of her jaw, her perfect warm smile enflaming all it touched. I was spellbound. We sat on the porch.

"Alright, who wants a drink?" I said in a show of fake bravado.

'Sure. I'll have one,' she said.

"It's champagne. I hope you don't mind."

"Fine by me. I'll have whatever's going."

As the alcohol flowed, so did our conversation. I can't for the life of me recall what we all talked about. The usual teenage conversations, as we all tried to impress one another with whatever anecdotes we could rustle up. I slipped into the increasingly familiar, warm glow of youthful inebriation and let my self-consciousness drift away like sand caught in the evening tide. My fears and my guarded teenage awkwardness melted away. She smiled. I made it my mission to make her smile again. It was a beautiful blur. Those hours of conversation took over my whole world in a way I had never experienced. It was a largely uneventful night. We left before midnight. I made sure I was home on time. But those fleeting moments when her smile was the direct product of something I had said gave me new purpose in life. I left completely dumbstruck yet floating with an intoxicant that far outweighed the simple fermented grapes swimming around my adolescent brain. I felt like she'd been plucked from some heavenly dream and shared with the world. I felt so lucky to have been able to bask in her glow for that brief moment. But even on that first meeting, I felt the deep psychological stabs, the pangs of longing, the deep truth that I knew I would never know her in the way I wanted, that I wasn't good enough, that I never would be.

We became friends. Her friends became our friends. We all hung out and our little group expanded. It was a very fun time. I had a huge circle of friends at this time in my life. As well as a really busy sporting schedule, there were so many parties and social gatherings going on. Every weekend there was something to do. Hanging out with friends when you're single and young and completely carefree has a lot of enticements, and besides, we all loved to drink. We all loved to get drunk.

Things for me on the school front were coming to a head. I had been at the same school since I was five years old. It was the school where my older brother had excelled and where I was foundering. The school where the junior school headmaster had described my brother as "book smart" and me as "street smart." I had given no evidence to the contrary. I had slid through whatever passes for primary education with the barest of care and with minimal effort. But I was stuck. I hated the school. I hated that it was all boys. I hated the culture of bullying, elitism, and snobbery that was the life-blood coursing through its blue veins. I wanted out. I began to get noticed in the only way I knew how. I began causing trouble. I stopped caring. I had become quite an experienced drinker already by fourteen. I would often help myself to the liquor cabinet when I got home from school. One recess I went home, drank something horrific, I think it was vermouth, and then went back to school. One of my classmates asked where I'd been and I told him.

"Whatever, you're so full of it," he piped at me.

"Come over after school. I'll show you."

"You're on," he arrogantly exclaimed.

"Good. I bet I can drink more than you." This again. What was wrong with me?

He came over. I poured us huge glasses of vermouth. We drank the entire bottle. It's not that strong, and I was drunk, but not massively. My friend seemed mostly fine too, so he went home looking a bit wobbly but generally okay.

That night I had been invited to another school's annual dance. I was keen to go and had scored myself some weed for the event so my friend and I could smoke it before we went in. Getting alcohol in there was a bit too risky but we had to get wasted somehow. We met at the train station close to the venue, then headed to the park and got very stoned.

"Hey man, I've got a joint. Want to smoke it?" I asked.

"Yeah dude. Sounds great."

"Let's head to the park and we can smoke it there."

"This dance thing is going to be pretty lame."

"Yeah, these things usually are."

"Why are we here again?"

"I don't know. Girls?"

"Oh yeah. All those girls we won't speak to." We laughed.

We went into the dance. I instantly regretted my decision to get stoned. I was so overwhelmed. I was also desperately trying to act cool by outwardly deriding the blaring Spice Girls that was pumping from the stereo when secretly inside I wanted to be dancing like a child possessed. I wish I'd danced the way I wanted to in my mind. We stood around awkwardly, as you do at those things, yearningly awaiting a time in life when these events would be an effortless breeze of charisma and charm. The holy grail of socializing that never occurs. It was in this rabbit hole of marijuana-soaked thought that I was abruptly brought back to the here and now by the presence of my mother who'd come to pick me up. She didn't look massively happy with me. I quickly exited, my cheeks flushing hot red. I got into the car.

"I've just been on the phone to the father of your friend from school, and he's been vomiting all afternoon. What did you boys do?"

"Nothing," I lied.

"Don't lie to me. He told his dad what you did. He said you had been drinking at our place." Well, so much for not ratting on me.

"Yeah, okay. We did. We came home after school before you and dad got home and we drank some of the booze in the cabinet."

I don't recall exactly what was said after that. But it involved a lot of disappointment. My poor parents, and they only knew the tiniest tip of the iceberg. The fact that I was sitting there listening to my mother, who I loved dearly and always have, say those things while I was high, while I still had weed in my pocket, after I'd let my friend poison himself on my parents' alcohol, it made me feel wretched. Even at that age, I had a conscience. I didn't want to be like this. I really didn't want to be the sort of kid who disappointed and let down their family repetitively. But unfortunately it was something I did regularly, and something I continued to do to my own family much later in life.

I changed schools the following year. I was so relieved to exit the utterly toxic environment of my previous school. The change of scenery was just what I needed. My grades improved.

I actually didn't mind going to school. But my circle of friends expanded yet again, and some more troubling elements crept back into my behavior. Amidst the genuine friendships there existed this very Australian attitude to alcohol. It was omnipresent. It was a culture of one-upmanship where reckless indulgence in booze showed everyone how cool you were. There was a time in the early days of senior school where we'd rotate smuggling small amounts of hard liquor into school in apple juice containers, which we'd consume on the oval at lunchtime. Many post-lunchtime classes were spent in a dull alcohol haze with my young brain swimming in intoxicants, the very antithesis of what education should be.

In between these brainless bouts of stupidity, I found myself reading a lot. I loved books. Our house was brimming with them. I sifted through my dad's science fiction collection. I read books on sailing, on surfing, on Roman history, on dinosaurs, crime fiction, short stories, poetry, anything I could get my hands on. It was a quiet and solitary pursuit. It was the refuge from the constant boundary pushing of the schoolyard. I sailed through this period of schooling, growing tired of messing up. I managed to keep out of trouble. Well, I didn't keep out of trouble, but I kept from getting caught. I kept my drinking to weekends and I got more and more into sport. But alcohol was cementing itself as a permanent and immovable feature of my life. It was the only way I knew how to socialize.

It's quite frightening to think, but between the ages of thirteen and thirty-six, when I finally gave up alcohol, I barely went a weekend without getting completely, toxically drunk. The period of my high school education in many ways laid the foundations of my adulthood as a high functioning binge drinker, later turned alcoholic. It was not anything particularly out of the ordinary and I'm sure many people reading this will see familiar stories of their own adolescence in these pages.

CHAPTER 5

When I was fifteen, I discovered that there are other drugs besides alcohol and weed at an intrepid individual's disposal. LSD was the most readily available and attractive drug at this time. I'm not sure what drew me to it: innocence? Adrenaline? Naivety? It was probably because my favorite bands were all heavily influenced by psychedelics, and as much as I wanted to be my own person, I was an impressionable youth. A much older friend of mine managed to procure some LSD. But where and how would we be able to do such a powerful drug? For starters, I had absolutely no idea what I was in for. None of us did. It was our school summer holidays and we had arranged a camping trip. It was a big deal for all of us. It was our first time away and unsupervised by our parents. It was a thrilling week of surfing and camping. I could not wait. It was also New Year's Eve and the thrill of what we imagined to be wild beach parties, full of potential, excited us all.

During this week, we all tried LSD for the first time. We meticulously and surgically cut the small tabs of paper in half and each sucked on our allotted segment of acid-drenched cardboard. We diligently performed this ritual and chased the odd, tingly-tasting sensation away with ice-cold beers. None of us had tried LSD before. None of us had any idea what was in store.

"Here you go, mate."

"Thanks," I replied.

"Don't swallow it. Just place it under your tongue until it dissolves. It'll kick in quicker."

"Yeah, cool. No worries."

"It'll be stronger too," he said with a slightly sinister smile.

"How do you know? You've never done it."

"No, but, well, that's what I was told."

"Yeah, cool. I'm just messing with you."

I placed the tab under my tongue and my stomach was all of sudden littered with butterflies.

We walked to the beach in search of some excitement. We gathered together. We walked. Down the dusty unpaved paths we travelled, each footstep elevating our heartbeats, heartbeats that pumped blood around our bodies, each breath in oxygenating our blood, pulsating chemicals around our system to where it was needed, each beat pushing the psychedelic chemical into our blood, into our brains, the subtle psychic properties began seeping into our youthful minds, each crunch of rock and dirt underfoot began to echo, each flicker of the pale street lamps lining the paths hung in our eyes that split second longer, light began refracting, the cellular nature of the entire natural world began to expose itself, a veil began to recede. No longer was the world a series of static whole entities. I began to see the world as a matrix, as an interconnected web in which my body and mind was enmeshed. I began to smile at the beauty and profound strangeness of it. We entered the beach. The mounds of sand shone in the moonlight. Each small ridge of sand taking on the otherworldliness of the moon, our torches the stellar beams of the ancient universe lighting up the beach in the most utterly transfixing ways. I stared at everything. Every mundane sight was dripping in beauty, holding me, capturing my gaze and thoughts. I began to laugh.

The conversations snapped me out of my trance. We started talking and the words came out as if of their own volition. Everything was funny. Everything was sidesplittingly hilarious. We finally ran into people. A group of much older people had a fire going and were drinking beers and having a bit of a party. We entered with extreme trepidation. We were kids. Kids on acid.

"What are you kids up to?" I was asked.

The strangeness of this question to my ears mixed with the thick, broad Australian accent made me burst out laughing. I couldn't control it. It just spewed out of me.

"What's wrong with you kids?" The voice rightly enquired. I couldn't control the laughter. It was so intense it hurt. I crawled off in fits of wild laughter tinged with embarrassment. We could not handle outside company. We had to retreat.

We left and walked back along the beach feeling like astronauts on some planet in the far reaches of space. It was dream-like, yet sharp and crystal clear. It was absurd and yet profound. It was lunacy and yet made utter sense. I felt as if I'd been psychically opened up and spoken to by nature, by God, by beauty itself, but it was also foggy and strange and riddled with doubt amongst a thin veil of sanity that felt on a precipice that could disintegrate at any point and leave me alone in a dark chasm of craziness.

This experience gave me a taste for psychedelics. But I failed to learn the most important lesson of drug taking. That first, profound experience is as good as it gets. It hits you so hard, and so effectively, that you fall in love with it. But that first time is the best. It's never as good again. The rest is just chasing that first moment of chemical intoxication. When the brain receives it for the first time. All other subsequent experiences are shadows, are simulations, wraiths of that magical authenticity of the first time. It sends you into the futile quest for the Holy Grail. The unachievable search for the magic from which you are now prohibited. Every person that has ever struggled with addiction knows this pang of longing. This lamenting longing for the Eden before we are expelled from the garden forever and left searching for it in the harsh wilderness.

The rest of my high schooling was a schizophrenic mix of sport, weekend binge drinking, occasional drug use and minimal schoolwork. It was fairly typical. We'd play sport on Friday nights and then head back to my friend's house and get a cask of wine and get absolutely hammered on cheap, rancid wine. Throughout this whole period my eyes never wavered from her. The same splendid being I had met and bonded with over stolen champagne. She played such an important role in my entire adolescence. I was besotted. But more than anything, I adored her.

I adored her company. I felt like the luckiest human just to be friends with her. I delighted in her company and died when she left. But the closeness I was so desperate for was always at arm's length. It could vanish with the snap of her fingers.

So many nights ended in deep frustration. Each party or gathering I went to with the faint hope that tonight would be different, that we'd finally admit that we both felt the same way about one another. I knew in my heart that she didn't. But her actions often belied a different truth. I called her.

"What do you want to do tonight?"

"I don't know. I don't think anything is on really."

"Where's everyone else?"

"Most of them are at a party."

"You didn't go?"

"I wasn't invited. Anyway, I was kind of hoping to catch up with you, if you're not busy?" I asked searchingly.

"I'm free. Want to come around and we can watch a movie?"

"Sounds good. I'll come over soon."

I grabbed my skateboard and undertook the twenty-minute journey from my house to hers. We chose a movie at the DVD store. It was the archaic time before Netflix. The movie we chose was a teen romantic comedy of some description, the ironic mirror of my own equally sappy teen drama that was unfolding in reality. I sat on the couch. Halfway into the movie, she came and sat next to me.

"Do you mind if I sit with you?"

"Of course. Come here."

She nestled into my lap. I began stroking her hair. This level of affection is clearly well beyond the realms of a strictly platonic friendship. I cherished these moments. It was what I so desperately wanted. But I could never seem to muster up the courage to put my feelings on the line.

"Hmm, that's really nice."

"I'm glad,' I replied, as I ever so gently ran the tips of my fingers along her hairline, along her beautiful forehead. She began looking as if she'd fall asleep.

"This is very relaxing. You have magic hands."

I laughed. I trembled. I looked at her face, resting peacefully against my chest, as her eyelids grew heavy and began to softly close. How I wanted to kiss those lips. I burned. But I froze. I just couldn't muster up the courage. The movie finished and she abruptly woke and stood up.

"I'm sorry. I fell asleep."

"It's okay. You're pretty cute when you're falling asleep."

"Don't tease me," she blushed.

"Just saying." I laughed.

"I'm actually really tired. I might go to bed. I've got heaps on tomorrow. Catch up tomorrow?"

"Um, yeah, of course. I'll head home." I tried to leave this statement open to see if there was any potential of an extended invite. Her mind was already somewhere else.

"Ok. Well, thanks for having me. Chat to you soon."

"Yeah, thanks for coming over," she replied.

We hugged. I held on to it, this closeness was all I'd ever wanted.

"Bye. Get home safe." I left.

It carried on like this for many years, too many episodes to recount, too many walks home alone, drunk, tired, yearning, wondering what was wrong with me, wondering why I wasn't good enough, feeling it was my looks, my mind, my words, all of which fell short, all of which was just not quite good enough.

And then, on my eighteenth birthday, we skirted dangerously close to the fire I knew would consume us if we let it. It went something like this...

A crystal clear, crisp, cool Saturday night in June ushered in my eighteenth birthday. I held a massive party at my parents' place. I had turned eighteen that day and could now legally buy alcohol. I bought beer, spirits, and three enormous ten-liter casks of wine. It was drastically over catered. But I always thought it was better to over cater than under cater. This party brought together all my diverse friendship groups and it was the first time my out of school friends mingled with my school friends. I was incredibly happy about this. It was all my favorite people at the time. We drank, we danced, and we partied. I was having such a wonderful time. I've never been shy of letting my now tall and lanky frame loose on the various dance floors in the dive bars that litter the dark corners of the world. I was drunk. Everyone was drunk. Half my buddies had taken acid. Half of them were just drinking. I refrained from the harder stuff and drank and danced with my schoolmates.

She brought her boyfriend. My heart sank. But I decided to ignore her as best I could and spent the evening dancing with some girls from school, both of who were friends, both of whom were completely uninterested in me beyond that friendship. We had a blast. We danced. We drank the cheap wine. We reveled in our youth. I savored my transition from child to adult by indulging in the childish ritual of bingeing on booze. All the while, I could feel the stares from the only person I'd ever wanted to stare at me like that. I could feel it searing hot in the cold winter air. The tension that I'd longed for built throughout the night. I threw myself into the party with the complete abandon that so often eluded me as my self-consciousness more often than not got the better of me. This shackle bent and broke. I let myself be my big dorky self. I let myself enjoy myself. I let myself be an adult and not care what others thought. I felt her gaze. I felt it truly for the first time.

She came over to me.

"I feel like I haven't seen you all night," she said, grabbing my arm.

"Yeah, I know. Sorry. Do you want to have a dance?"

"Yeah, sure." We danced. I felt the old familiar feelings of longing, yearning to be close to this person, shielding my eyes as her radiant beauty burnt my retinas. I tightened up. I got another drink.

"Are you okay?" She asked. "It feels like you've been avoiding me all night."

"Yeah, I'm fine. I'm sorry if I've been avoiding you. I didn't mean to. Where's your boyfriend?"

"He left a while back," she said with a timid, embarrassed curl of her upper lip.

"It's really nice to see you with all your friends," she said, awkwardly.

"What do you mean?"

"I mean, like, you know, dancing and having fun…flirting."

"Flirting?" I exclaimed.

"Yeah, flirting. As if you're not flirting with them." She glanced her eyes towards my two school friends with a minute veiled flash of jealousy in her eyes.

"Oh come on. We're not flirting. We're all just buddies."

"Well, it looks like they're pretty into you."

"They're so not," I retorted. They so weren't.

"Well, make sure you save me a dance later, okay?"

"Sure. Always."

I went and found more booze. The party got looser. I got far drunker. I continued to dance and revel with my friends. But the night started to wind down, as they always do. My mates who'd taken acid left with their brains dribbling out their ears. A few random people had vomited. Some had hooked up. Almost all had left. As I said goodbye to the remaining guests, I noticed that she had lingered.

I was glad. We often hung out after everyone left, after everyone had gone to bed, or passed out. It was part of our friendship. The post party debrief where I staved off the creeping specter of sleep to milk every single minute with her, to be in her presence, to have her to myself for that extra moment in the quiet after the chaos of teenage parties.

She came over to me.

"You still owe me that dance."

"Yeah, I do."

I grabbed her waist timidly and started swaying with the lingering vestige of alcohol rocking us gently on the tide. So much was always unspoken. So many opportunities for an expression of the truth of my feelings buried beneath insecurity, beneath fear, and painful self-awareness, from a lack of faith, a lack of daring. How could one person betray himself so obviously to everyone with his actions and yet keep his words locked so far from sound?

"I was actually quite jealous seeing you dance with those girls tonight."

"Why's that?" I asked, my voice starting to tremble.

"I was just dancing."

"Those girls were really into you," she said.

"I don't think so."

"Why didn't you kiss any of them?" she asked.

"Do you really need me to answer that?" I stared straight into the grey pools of her magnificent eyes as I said these words. Sadly, it was the closest I ever came to telling her how I really felt.

We kissed. The warm, sweet, impossibly soft contours of her lips pressed against mine. The world ground to a halt. Time froze. I put my hands around her waist and pressed her to me. I had longed for this moment for so many years. I enveloped her small frame in my arms and embraced my friend in the arms of pure love. It was utterly electrifying. We embraced and kissed for a long time. We finally broke our entwining.

"I have to go. Um, happy birthday." She left.

The next day, I awoke with my head pounding from the liters of cheap wine I'd drunk. I thought I had a bad hangover, but I'd later find the true meaning of hangovers when I hit my thirties and starting mixing amphetamines in to the alcohol broth. I called my friend. We'd kissed. This was it. It was happening. Finally. She answered the phone.

"Hello."

"Hi. It's me."

"Oh. Hi. How are you feeling?" What a question. Where could I start?

"Um. Okay. Pretty hung over. But not too bad considering. How are you?" The small talk slipped out of my mouth and its utterance was as if sharp nails were being scraped down a blackboard. Tell her.

"Um, yeah, I'm fine, I guess," she responded in a puzzling tone.

"What's up?"

"Oh, nothing. Well, um, I broke up with my boyfriend this morning."

My blood quickened, my heart beat faster, the pores on my forehead began to release tiny beads of sweat, this might actually happen.

"Oh, you did? Why?" I asked.

"I didn't think it was fair given last night."

"Last night. Yeah," I responded, dying to tell her all the things I had felt for her for so long. My tongue wouldn't work. I froze.

"Um, about that. It was a mistake."

"Oh. Okay." My voice trembled as my stomach sank and my heart disintegrated.

"Yeah, it was really nice, but I don't want to jeopardize our friendship."

"No. That would be bad." I didn't know what else to say. I was crushed.

"Yeah, I just love you so much and would hate to complicate things. We're too good as friends," she said persuasively.

The door was shutting. I did everything I could to hold back the utter despair that gripped me in that moment.

"And, you know, I just don't want things to get awkward between us."

"No, of course not. They never would," I said.

"I knew you'd understand. You're such a good friend."

"Yeah, um, you too."

"Okay, great. Thanks for, you know, understanding. I'll chat to you soon."

"Yeah. Speak soon."

I hung up the phone, the weight of rejection bearing down on me and compounding my already severe hangover. I grabbed a glass, filled it with the remnants of the wine cask, went to my room and drank alone until I passed out.

After managing to keep my feelings completely hidden in all but words, the girl of my dreams left. She went and stayed away for years. Many years. We kept in touch. I couldn't believe how much I missed her. It was like a huge part of me was just gone. As much as I wanted things to progress and for us to become a proper couple, more than anything, I really missed my friend. We were so close. Life was pulling us in completely different directions. I still wrote drunken poetry about her. I still came home alone at the end of every massive drug and booze session and dreamed about the day she'd come home. Home to me. To my arms. To my kisses. To my undying affection. I still scribbled the resentment and hurt I bore through countless pages of a worn-out old notebook, writing with the entitled desperation of a drunken lunatic. I poured my teenage angst out in an attempt to grow and be rid of it. Alcohol fueled the cathartic scribbling, but it prevented me from processing much of it. I missed my friend. I longed for the closeness we'd never achieve. Alcohol did nothing to help me deal with any of it. It trapped me in a suppression cycle, but it was the only coping strategy I knew. At eighteen I had already laid the foundation of booze as my only means to cope with the universal struggles of teenage existence like acceptance, self-worth, and unrequited love. I didn't know how to feel and not fall back on alcohol to handle those feelings.

CHAPTER 6

As much as I'm an idiot, I'm also really not. I knew when to work. I knew when effort was required and I knew that some things are more important than a hedonistic romp. My final year of school was the one shining light of my adolescence. I never stopped drinking on weekends. Despite my weekend binges and occasional solitary depression riddled abuses of alcohol, I got through my schooling much better than I, or anyone, ever expected. I got a very high grade point average and graduated near the top of my year. I had my pick of universities and colleges. But I was so unsure about what to do next. I decided to apply for a Bachelor of Arts at a prestigious local university. I was accepted and promptly deferred so I could "find myself." What a cliché. But this year was great in a lot of ways. I turned my hand at many things, odd jobs, sport, windsurfing instructing, gyms, pools, and of course, lots of drinking. I went to Maui, Hawaii for a few months chasing a dream to become a professional windsurfer. This was amazing. I'd never been healthier or fitter. I spent the entire day in the water every day. I had a good group of friends, and being under the legal drinking age combined with spending most of my time with non-drinkers worked wonders in keeping me out of trouble. But I got bored. I was a city slicker at heart. I returned home to the lure of the nightlife, to the lure of friends, to the lure of the people I loved, to the lure of the woman I still loved despite my best efforts.

I decided to study history and literature and indulge my love of books that I'd had since I was a kid. I did well enough. I enjoyed study enormously. But in my twenties, I began to spiral into the world of amphetamines and party drugs. Every weekend was awash with drugs and alcohol. In between drug-fueled benders, alcohol was increasingly featuring as my emotional and psychological crutch to get through the comedowns. Again, throughout this period in my life I somehow managed to get through university. But I also had some hideous experiences. Only with time and retrospection have I realized just how precarious my existence was. This phase of my life was extreme.

Alcohol had become such a feature of social interactions by this point that I had forgotten what we all used to do before it. I had also been drinking solidly for six years and the drug had embedded itself in my social activities. More than that it had quickly become my crutch, my salve, my daily safety blanket to shelter me from all life's harsher edges. While alcohol would never truly leave my side for the next eighteen years, it was about to get a boost from the engine room of amphetamines.

I had tried ecstasy at a party, years before when I was fourteen. It didn't do anything at all. I think it was chalk. I'm just glad it wasn't rat poison, as I'm fairly sure I've ingested my fair share of that over the years. At an end of year school dance in my sophomore year, I tried real ecstasy for the first time. That was an entirely different story. Cool waves of calm serenity descended over my mind. All fears, doubts, worries, insecurities, melted away, like footprints left etched in the sand now washed away with the increasing ocean tide. My brain lit up like a dopamine Christmas tree. Contentedness, calm, happiness, warmth towards everything emanated from my every thought. It was so peaceful, so fun. I had such a wonderful night. I thought it was going to last forever, all from half a small pill. As the sun rose, the feeling of never ending energy and compassion began to wane. I went home after a blurry kiss with one of my school friends.

The next day however taught me a valuable lesson in the true nature of drugs. The horror of coming down from that much serotonin flooding my brain was brutal. Even at seventeen, it hurt so badly. I felt like I had destroyed my brain. I was sad. I was angry. I was moody, despondent, and I felt so very far away from the warm gooey pile of compassionate mush I was the night before. I felt jagged and hard. I felt like the rock ledges that the seething stormy oceans batter day in and day out to form sand. I am rock. I am being beaten to sand. I thought to myself that it just isn't worth it. And it wasn't. I didn't touch it again until after I'd finished school.

But after school had finished and I'd moved out of home, the weekend pull of binge drinking and drugs were strong. Drugs were a more and more prominent feature of my weekends, and alcohol, as ever was its criminal partner in chaos. Not only was I using alcohol heavily before and during the weekend drug binges, but it was also all too easy to turn to the accessible arms of alcohol to ease the transition back from the drug-fueled mania of any given weekend.

This started when I was nineteen. I was at the twenty-first birthday party of a really close friend. We managed to procure a solid amount of MDMA, as we always did. The night was a relative blur. We all got high. The cool waves rushing over our psyches as the warm glow of ecstasy flushed our cheeks red and loosened our tongues to explore any of the vapid, meaning-less thoughts of gooiness that flitted up from our sub-conscious. It's an attractive sensation. I'd be lying if I said there isn't a part of me that misses this type of abandon. But what ecstasy does, more than anything, is to just make everything "nice." To anyone slightly anxious, insecure, unsure of themselves (i.e. pretty much everyone) it just removes those hard edges and smothers them in a fluffy pink pillow. It's very enticing. It makes every night a nice night. But although we all talked our faces off until the sunrise, no one laughs on MDMA. We talk, we touch, we feel weight, gravity, depth of love and tenderness, but humor is gone. It evaporates, because humor requires hard edges. It requires that which is uncanny. Humor is dark. It's based on our senses of irony, of playfulness, our flirtation with our inner maudlin, macabre selves. Ecstasy removes all of that because it's just nice. Nice isn't funny. So after an epic night of humorless, deep conversing, I finally retreated home in the shameful hours of early daylight. Skulking through my suburban street to collapse on my bed, alone, again, my jaw sore from clenching, from chattering, from talking endless drivel, all to stave off the reality of sleeping in my bed alone. Always alone. I checked my phone to see any promising glimpse of her. Silence.

I woke up after few hours of terrible amphetamine-addled sleep. I usually owned my hangovers, particularly when I was younger. I had this idea that I had dug myself into the pit and I had to suffer my way out of it. No paracetamol, no ibuprofen, no booze, no weed. Suck it up. Well, it turns out that was fairly short-lived. I cracked a bottle of wine and drank the whole thing. The wine helped. It kind of reactivated the latent chemicals still floating around. From that point on, I often drank to alleviate comedowns. As I got older the alcohol became more and more the crutch that I leant on to get myself out of the weekend's pit. But it just delayed everything. You still have to go through the post party blues. It's a slippery slope. Drinking to avoid comedowns. Drinking to avoid hangovers. It's addiction in motion. It's how we progress our addictions. It's ultimately not too long before we enter into the perpetual cycle of being drunk or hung over, and more and more, I felt that drinking was the perfect hangover cure. Instead, it's the precipice of the cliff of alcohol dependence.

The next few years were completely awash with partying. Every weekend without fail, I would not sleep at least one night of the weekend. These nights would always begin the same way. We'd start with "a few beers somewhere." Even when I had no intention of having a big bender, the minute alcohol hit my brain, my decision-making faculties crumbled. Once such night began with a few beers…

My friends were all attending a rave in bush land about two hours' drive from Melbourne. This was the era of small dance parties in the bush. They were often without permits and had no facilities whatsoever. It was also in the days before the cops could do drug testing, so we'd often drive up, get high, not sleep and drive home. Sometimes, there was someone who could actually drive. More often, one of us would drive high. We almost never drove drunk though. That was supposed to make it all better. Some friends of mine were attending one such event. I decided not to go. So I went to the local pub for a few beers with a mate. We got stuck into the drinks. We must have had at least ten beers each. But the drinks weren't hitting the spot. I had a deeper thirst. I hankered for something stronger. But the only place I knew where to find it was at this outdoor rave.

"Want to go find them all?" I asked, half jokingly.

"Yeah, I kind of do," he replied, tentatively.

We jumped in the car. I drove. Drunk. Out into the forest. Using an old map. This was pre-smartphones, so we had to stop and check the map quite regularly. Drunk. A cop car passed us. I did everything I could to stay straight. The cops might not yet have the technology to test for drugs, but they sure could test for alcohol. They sped off, completely uninterested in us.

We drove on. Silently. My eyelids started to grow heavy at the lack of alcohol topping up the increasingly stale feeling of an impending hangover. It was after midnight. We drove on. Bitumen turned to unpaved roads. Unpaved roads turned to dirt tracks. Through the grim silence of Victorian bush I could now start to hear the maniacal throbbing of bass. The pulsing pull of electronic music in the darkness of the forest. We followed my map and could now hear the unmistakable sounds of the party. We arrived. It was small. We found our friends quickly and effortlessly. I bought drugs. I had them before the transaction was even complete.

"I thought you weren't coming," said a friend.

"I wasn't." I grinned back at him with the cheeky smile of someone who has just gotten away with something.

"I don't want to know how you got up here, man."

"I drove. Stupid, I know. But I'm here," I replied, sheepishly. "You're an idiot."

"Yeah, I know." I was genuinely contrite.

"I'm glad you're here anyway, man."

"Have you got any beers?" I asked.

"Of course buddy. Here you go."

We sat down and the pills kicked in. We sat there in those seats talking until the sun rose over the stunning forest hills in the foreground. We got up and had a dance. The morning dance, off our faces on ecstasy, was always the highlight of these parties. The energy of the amphetamine drove us hard into the beat of ridiculously fast electronic techno. But these parties were full of freaks and social misfits, just as they were full of future doctors and lawyers. It was a cross section of society where the strictures and regulations, cliques, and boundaries of normal society didn't apply. In my most romantic images of these events, I see a beautiful dissolution of pretense, primal movement in the sea of our common humanity. In my more cynical moments, I see a bunch of us wallowing in cheap, dangerous escapism. The seedy underbelly of drug deals and organized crime only ever a small scratch of the fingernail from the thin surface of freedom, dance, and self-expression. I guess it's both. The worlds and lives of most humans are capable of being multiple things at once. These parties certainly, for me, ran the gamut of intensely liberating, to stiflingly contradictory, hypocritical and just plain seedy.

I drove home with enough amphetamines in my system for me to think I was still awake. I drove in a fog, and I can't remember it. I can't remember clearly getting home. But I did. I went to my room and slept for 16 hours. I awoke again in a chasm of regret, my severely serotonin-depleted brain reeling at the sheer stupidity of driving whilst under the influence of both alcohol and then amphetamines. But this wasn't an isolated incident.

All nights, no matter how big or small, started with one drink. Alcoholics Anonymous are very adamant that once you are cursed with alcoholism, it is a life-long affliction that means you can never drink again. It's a hard line. It's not one many of us can accept when we first decide to address our drinking. When I started with One Year No Beer, I was really taken by the softer approach. It was more about changing our relationship with alcohol. That was something I had always wanted to do. Even back then in the grips of my partying, a small yet annoyingly incessant voice scolded me for my drinking. I always knew it was problematic. If I had known then what I know now about how hard quitting would be I might have thought twice. If I had known how many years I was going to keep making the same mistake, time and time again, I like to think I would have taken action earlier. Don't let it get too far. All of us that drink too much know we shouldn't. We know we drink too much. We have our conscience there warning us. All I can say is that if this is you, if you are someone like me, who in the grips of revelry, who in the grips of cocktails that get out of hand, who in the grips of pints with the boys, who in the grips of a two day bender that results in you sniffing cocaine off toilet cisterns in disgustingly unhygienic night club toilets, then you are most certainly not alone. We are not alone in these struggles. The worst thing we can do is to isolate ourselves and tell ourselves we're abnormal, or wrong, or deviant, or stupid, or weak. We are none of those things. Many of us have battled with drinking and drugs and done really amazing things in life. We are operating with half a deck of cards and still kicking butt. Some of us aren't. Some of us are getting far along enough on this dark road that it's consuming us. None of us are alone in this. We're here. People from all walks of life battle addiction. We battle with booze. We battle with drugs, food, body image, gambling, and with all manner of things. All we can do is to talk about it and not suffer in the shadows. No one wins in that scenario.

CHAPTER 7

The reveler's shame:

"Red wine-stained lips and yellow finger tips, conver-sations on repeat, repeat, talking, talking, everyone's talking, no-one's listening everyone speaking, over and over, over each other, over themselves, over his-tory, over time, tripping on speech, tripping on limbs, slurred words, stories on repeat, repeat, empty bot-tles, heady smoke hanging, dense evening air, people, people everywhere, no air only heat, humid, dank, city grime gets under fingernails, gets under eyelids, flows into lungs, seeps into blood, escapes through sweat, hearts quicken, pupils dilate, empty promises pull us in, the descent, down through bluestone stairs,

through cellar doors, past neon signs, away from the open star-filled sky, low ceilings, where glasses clink, registers ring, cash handed over, gone, the recompense for our loss of time, ends up in filthy toilets, flushed, gone, repeat, repeat, back on the street, lights blur, eyes squint, bustling, a city's exodus in the small hours before dawn, drivers ferry the victims of inebriation's grip, the thankless tasks, repeat, repeat, neon starlight, the tree lined streets soften under the first licks of sunlight's dawn, a brief moment of silence, brief refrain, no people on the dead end streets, just the lost children of the reveler's delights, the reveler's curse, the reveler's shame, the reveler's shame, repeat, repeat." Drew Charles – June, 2019

In my final year of my undergraduate degree I was doing a double major in history and English. English was exciting, crazy, and I got exposed to the literature that both broke my mind open, and the literary figures such as Hunter S. Thompson, Thomas Pynchon, and Kathy Acker that I used to legitimize my raging partying. So, rewind to that pivotal time…

We were already drunk. We entered the club. People started pouring in. We headed to the bar. We drank, and as we did so, we swallowed a tab of acid and a capsule of MDMA. We drank. The music begun to throb with intensity, as the crowd swelled, the chemical tide came in and drowned the final pathetic murmurings of my inhibitions. Cool waves of euphoria surged, the steady monotonous pulse of the nightclub started beating to the same consistent warm flutters of my heart. We danced through the night and finally spilled out of the club into the frosty Melbourne morning. Too wired to sleep, too crippled with LSD to function. I called my mate.

"Man, it's 8am. What do you want?" He sounded rather annoyed with me.

"Mate, we're on the tear. Want to come party?"

"Man, are you serious? What have you been up to?"

"We went to an indoor party and, well, we partied." I broke into maniacal laughing.

"You crazy kids. I'll get dressed and come over."

"Oh, and buddy, bring some goodies if you have any." I said, trying to be cryptic.

"Yeah bud, I'll bring what I have."

We left the city, the slumbering steel giant receded in the mirror as our poor cab driver listened to two people that clearly sounded certifiably insane even to my ears, and I was doing the majority of the talking. I tipped the cabbie heavily, poor dude. We arrived at my house. My housemate was thrilled to be woken up first thing on Sunday morning to the dulcet tones of large, completely annihilated idiots being "quiet" through fits of uncontrollable laughter. I bribed him with beers. He was cool with it in about ten minutes.

My other mate arrived.

"Well, I'm here. Where are my beers?"

"Cheeky." I gave him a hug and got him a beer. The walls were melting.

"I brought what you're after, fellas."

We poured out huge lines of speed and snorted them. The intense, barely cut crystals carved out my nasal passage like a searing hot knife cauterizing a wound. Pain gave way to rushes of manic, euphoric energy.

More people arrived, and a full-blown day party ensued. This extended well into the night. Poor neighbors. I finally booted everyone out, the house wearing the scars of reckless abuse, its savage griminess the perfect mirror of my internal state. It was nearly dawn on Monday morning. As much as I didn't want to admit it, this was an every weekend occurrence.

But I had an assignment due that day. I tried to sleep. I was somehow still wired. I got up and wrote the assignment, flitting in and out of varying states of delirium. The essay got written. I printed it out and began the shameful trip to the campus to hand it in, a deathly shadow through busy downtown Melbourne. I wanted to crawl into a hole and die. My essay was by far the worst thing I have ever handed in at university. It passed and did what it needed to do. I thought I was so clever for getting away with this for many years.

I missed the point of this episode until I recently. The point of learning isn't grades. It isn't what you can get away with. It isn't about sliding, fluking your way through everything while you yourself act like a complete train wreck. It's about expanding your mind, extending your brain and pushing the boundaries of what's cognitively comfortable in order to give yourself additional dimensions. I thought I was doing that through drug experiences, and maybe sometimes that might have been true. But more and more it looked like I was just feeding addictions and post-rationalizing them after the event because I was scraping by. How much can one person get in their own way before the penny drops? When I finally made the decision to get sober, it was fueled by the desire to not scrape by anymore. I also didn't want to get hung up on the metrics of western life: weight, salary, grades, it's just as misguided as searching for meaning in the bottom of a glass, or a zip-lock bag. So in a strange way after all my education, sobriety felt like the desire for real learning. My experience of sobriety eventually showed me what holistic learning actually looks like. But the lessons I needed to heed would not begin to sink in for many years yet.

In this period of crazy partying I was lucky enough to meet the woman who would later become my wife. The first night I met her, I was completely sideways. I'd been drinking all day, and decided to head to a nightclub with my mates. We had a bag of pure MDMA (the main chemical in ecstasy), and we quickly made our way through it.

I met her. I was instantly drawn to the stunning beauty of her sweet smile. The way she moved on the dance floor was utterly transfixing. But the warmth of her face was what held me. I was captivated. I thought of so many things I could say to her. My jumbled synapses, my true thoughts, the real me was buried in a sea of alcohol and ramble-inducing MDMA. My mouth disconnected from my brain and began talking to her about all kinds of rubbish. I told her about my girlfriend at the time who I knew wasn't right for me. I told her at length about the intricacies of my family. Why on Earth would she be interested in that? I couldn't stop talking drivel. It just kept pouring out of me. She started trying to avoid me, and rightly so. She finally buckled under my dribbling stupidity.

"Look, mate. I came here to dance."

Yes. She did. What was I here for? To yell over the loudest indoor electronic music I'd ever experienced? To ear bash a stranger about every little thought I was having as I was having them? Smooth. In my defense, which is flimsy at best, I just wanted to be around her. I couldn't not be. Even then, I knew I wanted her in my life. The hard bit was going to be to convince her I wasn't a complete idiot. I left the club with my mates and we continued to smash drugs all day. I was still so struck by my meeting with my future wife. Although I made the worst possible first impression, she did the exact opposite. Her image was burned into my brain, and it refused to diminish. And as I write this nearly twenty years after that chance meeting, her image burns as brightly and as strongly as ever.

It was really not my best effort in impressing her. I was an idiot. I thought of it all too often. I was so embarrassed that I'd been that guy. Oh well. But chance meetings are sometimes destined to occur again. Luckily for me, I had a chance to redeem myself only a few short months later at an electronic music festival.

The next time I met her, I was sober. It was at a bush rave a few hours north of Melbourne. I arrived, and was reintroduced by a friend. I apologized for my performance at our previous meeting. We started chatting. The awkward timidity of first meetings flooded both our cheeks hot red. But despite our jitters, the conversation flowed. I stole glances into the utterly entrancing, deep, calm, and serene pools of her rich, compassionate eyes. The soothing, mellow tones of her voice a constant contrast to the obnoxious din of the music at the festival, her smooth pale skin glowing like a nocturnal angel's in the deep dark of the Australian bush. The flickering of her eyes dancing with starlight, sharing flashes of the inner radiance I'd come to know and fall in love with.

I had a bag of drugs in my pocket and we shared them. The night from then was nothing short of intoxicating. We barely stopped to draw breath until the sun started to streak the outback Australian sky, dusting it a pale pink before the long strands of golden beams licked the wheat fields, swaying hypnotically in the warm summer breeze.

But the first two hours, those magic hours, where we were both fully present, fully aware, before we launched into the contents of my pockets, those hours, I will never forget. We were both seeing other people at the time, so we did nothing but talk. But the connection was formed at that meeting. The drugs and booze that followed were irrelevant. I always feared that the drugs were the glue that bound us. But they weren't. It was the brief experience of being sober together that revealed who we really were to one another. And I've never forgotten, despite repeatedly smacking myself in the head with a drug and booze brick every weekend for years after that night. The truth of the realization that we adored each other sober eventually came to the surface when I finally got sober. It only served to strengthen our relationship, as I was finally reliable. What I said and what I did started to align. That takes a lot of pressure off our partners.

As the sun came up, she sensibly went to bed. I took acid, speed and more pills, and partied nonstop for the next two days. I was yet to learn the most valuable and striking lesson of that weekend almost twenty years ago. And I wouldn't for many, many years. But I'm learning now. Sometimes I stay home. Even on the rare occasions she decides to go out. Some nights,

I don't feel robust enough to venture into the sites of my old life. Sometimes I feel like I can't handle another night amongst drunk people, amongst stoned people, another night, yet another night, saturated in booze, saturated in the past, saturated in the temptations of the path to my future misery. Sometimes, I am able to cope, other times, I cannot. I take heed of my instincts now, and if they're telling me to stay in, I listen.

CHAPTER 8

By the time I was in my mid twenties, I was starting to grow tired of the never-ending partying. Every weekend, it was the same routine. Routines of anything, even crazy partying, can turn into drudgery. I decided I needed a change of scenery. I moved to the other side of Melbourne. I moved to be close to the water and next door to my amazing sister. The water was always my great solace in life. I'd always been immersed in the ocean at any opportunity. My dad and my older brother got me into surfing and windsurfing as a child. I have really fond memories of hanging out with both of them, sailing, surfing, having fun and being free in the water. That time in the ocean was really my salvation in between bouts of drunkenness and through the troughs between parties. So I decided to move away from the parties and get closer to the beach, close to my sister, away from chaos and hopefully towards some calm. Things are never this linear, but my exodus from the north of Melbourne did curb my partying for a time. I also had two major projects emerging that began to fill my time. The first was my doctorate in literature. The second was music.

The doctorate was a lonely, solitary and isolating pursuit. I loved it for that. Hours spent in the solitary confinement of the library basement, pouring through old journals, it was my idea of intellectual heaven. No interaction, very few distractions, and one big piece of work to get my teeth into. It was the most challenging of tasks. But I enjoyed it, was broken by it, recovered to complete it, and finally received my doctorate with what remained of the tatters of my sanity. Throughout this whole mountainous academic trial, I drank heavily. It felt completely natural to dust off a hangover by going to the library and attempt to undo some of the neural damage from the preceding evening by poring through some esoteric nonsense that would or wouldn't make it to my own equally obscure piece of eccentric literary criticism. Red wine and dusty books, being a part of the sarcastic, cynical, drunken literati had a definite romanticism. But I kept my head out of the clouds, and my brain in the gutter by my experience in the music scene. This was a blessing and a curse. I felt at the time that the wonderful creative endeavor of being in bands was the crucial antidote to the stuffy world of the academy. But at the same time, being in bands drastically increased my exposure to the kind of lifestyle I was trying to avoid.

The struggles of bands are many. It's well documented in far more interesting ways than I can tell you. The bands I played in all had their moments of varying low-level successes. Success is a largely subjective concept, but all bands that record music are huge successes in my eyes. The ability to have created something that didn't exist before is what artistic activities are all about. I played in one band with my dear friend and we had some success in the electronic music scene and played some big festivals. I had some big shows with another incredibly close friend, but our band was more focused on song writing and we have recorded some music I am intensely proud of, even though it never got much attention. Every weekend we'd meet at 9am on Saturday morning to write and record music in our makeshift studio. We wrote so many songs. We recorded so many songs, not particularly well, but it was enough to hear what we'd done and refine what we were trying to do. It kept me out of trouble and his friendship is one I will treasure forever.

In 2012, I began playing in a new band. It began like this:

"Hey mate, I'm thinking of putting a new band together. Can I send you some demos?"

"Sure. I'd love to hear them." I was in New York at the time, dusting off the cocaine and alcohol of the preceding evening. I listened. I called back.

"Mate, they sound brilliant. Should we have a jam and see how we go?"

We had a jam. We booked our first show after that one rehearsal. The show was a bit of a mess. But it was a really fun mess. I loved playing with those guys. That's how our band was born. No fear. No let up, just frantic energy to be doing things, perpetual motion, even to our own detriment. We played hundreds of shows in our first year together. At one point we were playing four nights a week just in Melbourne. We recorded. We released music. That music was played on the radio. We toured. I drank. I started to drink at every gig. Every show ended in a blur of intoxication. At this point, I only drank heavily after the gigs. I was putting on a flimsy cloak of professionalism. We kept playing, kept touring, and after the dust settled on an already whirlwind first year, we recorded our debut album.

At this point, the whole process was so much fun. We drove ten hours to play shows to 30 people. We just didn't care. We loved playing. We loved each other. We loved music. It didn't matter if there were 10 people or 1000, we played like we were at Madison Square Garden every time we hit the stage. I remember distinctly having this conversation with the guys on one of our many long drives:

"I remember seeing this band. They came over from Perth to play at the Workers Club. There were two people and myself in the audience. They just played their hearts out. They didn't care how many people were there. They just did what they do for the love of it."

"That's so awesome. I love seeing bands going for it and not relying on how many people are there to see it," I replied.

"That's what we're about too, man."

"I think so too. I guess the minute we stop buzzing from playing to an empty room, then it's time to call it a day." Playing music to empty rooms did eventually stop being fun. But the love between us had also gone. I don't know which left first.

Our debut album landed and we got some very modest success. But we were touring relentlessly and we were starting to really sizzle as a live band. I started applying for some events.

We ended up playing South by Southwest in Austin, Texas. For those of you that don't know, this is the biggest music festival and conference in the world and is a rite of passage for many emerging bands. It's a big opportunity to strut your stuff in front of the world's music industry. It felt like a big deal. We also managed to get our album onto college radio in the States where it charted as high as number fourteen. We got booking agents at home and abroad. Things started to look like they might finally work for us as musicians.

We reveled in it all. The other guys were insatiable front men and absolute characters. They were recognized everywhere they went. They had style and mystique and an ability to get in the limelight and thrive in the attention. I was not like this at all. I was the shy lanky dude at the back. On stage, behind the safety of a drum set, I'd let my performing side fully out and unleash on my instrument. I cared deeply about drums. I practiced. I studied. I wanted to be as good as I could. I wanted each show to be better than the last. But I'm a nervous, anxious performer. When I started playing shows I'd often vomit beforehand purely from nerves. I also hated posing for photographs. I hated the self-promotion that is inescapably necessary for any success in music. I hated having to greet people before shows, to lean on people to come, to spend every spare second on social media hustling for numbers to shows. I hated it, but I also wanted it so badly. I worked myself into knots about it. I started drinking more and more to cope with the ever-increasing anxiety that raising the stakes started to precipitate.

I started to get so anxious before shows. I particularly struggled with things completely outside my control like who would

turn up and how many people would come. I'd drink to alleviate that anxiety. It was the only coping mechanism I knew. But
then I'd feel like I'd drunk too much to play well and start to
get anxious about that. So rather than not drink, I began trying
to source amphetamines to "sober me up" before shows. Dexamphetamine was the preference. Failing that, I'd use speed if
I could. If that was impossible to source, cold and flu tablets
would work. Worst-case scenario, I'd have two Red Bulls. It's
all probably equally damaging. It was all a futile attempt to dig
up out of a hole of my own making. Not getting in the booze
hole in the first place would make more sense. But the uppers
to get over my drunkenness meant that after the show, I was
always completely charging. This would lead to more beers,
more drugs, and more often than not, partying all night and all
the next day. It is a cycle. It is really hard to break.

We had a really big couple of shows supporting a sold-out
tour featuring a member from a much more famous band. I
was so nervous. There was preshow drama about equipment.
There's always preshow drama of some description. The promoter was a charlatan and had managed to deeply offend the
headline act. Of course, more often than not, I took this on to
try and fix it. I let them use my drum kit. We always ended up
bending over backwards to help others. Many times, this was
to our own detriment. These acts are rarely reciprocated. Yet I
never seemed to learn my lesson. I was anxious. I drank. Luckily, I'd been given some Dexies. I drank more than I should,
to blur the stress, to smudge the harsh edges. Whatever excuse
I could muster to hide the fact that alcohol and anxiety were
fast becoming inextricable bedfellows. I'd get anxious. I'd get

drunk. Drunkenness alleviates the anxiety in the moment. But it's a hideous spiral.

"Hey mate, the headline band needs to use your drum kit and all your amps," the promoter directs me.

"I thought there was going to be drums and amps provided."

"I don't remember saying that."

"It's in the email you sent around."

"Oh. Well, there was an issue with the delivery of it and they weren't able to get it here on time. So, all the bands need to use your gear," he responded bluntly.

"Fine," I responded tersely. I walked away in disgust and head straight to the bar.

"Hey man, you okay?"

"Yeah, I'm fine. I just am getting a bit sick of always getting walked all over by these promoters."

"Here you go, mate." I am handed several pills.

"Thank you. I really need these."

I took all three Dexies at once. I didn't even flinch. I chased them with a large gulp of my beer. I took to the stage. I took out all my frustration and resentment at our treatment by the promoter on my drum kit. We lit up the stage. We played like our lives were on the line. We threw ourselves around the stage as if the music within us could only express itself in some kind of fit, some mad, full body convulsion born of fire and pure combustive energy. The drugs, the beers, the manic energy of performance, it's a powerful cocktail. I came off stage absolutely charging. We made a straight line for the bar. Some mates were there.

"That was sick, dude. Great show."

"Thanks man. Thanks so much for coming."

"Want a line?"

"You know it."

We headed to the toilet and poured cocaine out onto the black mirror of my mobile phone. Before I inhaled, that ever present, dim voice in the back of my mind piped up to ask me again, "What are you doing?" The voice receded. Desire took over. I snorted the drugs.

"Thanks so much, mate. I needed that." I didn't need that. I never really needed to sniff cocaine in dirty toilets after already consuming amphetamines and alcohol. I never really needed more stimulation after playing a great set of rock and roll to a full house of people. These are just the myths I spun to justify my desires. When we desire drugs, we make the myth suit the desired action. I did it every time. I honestly told myself I needed it, and that I deserved it. But those myths are surface. Their veneer is so thin. Paper-thin. Below it is the harsher voice that echoes the sentiment of me deserving it, but for an entirely different reason: I deserve this, because I am worthless. I deserve the outcomes of my behaviors because I am weak. I am a mess. I am useless. I am nothing. I partied all night. I stayed out all night.

My phone rang. It was my wife.

"Hello darling, how are you?" I said, trying not to sound trashed.

"Where are you?"

"I'm still out."

"Have you slept?"

"No."

"Eaten?"

"No."

"Man. You could have called."

"I know. Sorry." Silence.

"How's your morning been?"

"Fine. Worried. But fine otherwise." This was getting icy. Guilt was creeping in through the haze of drug and alcohol remnants. Why did I keep doing this to her? To myself?

"I can come and get you, if you like? You have to be ready now though," she said, her voice sounding conciliatory enough.

"Okay. That would be great. Ready when you are."

She picked me up from my mate's house.

"Thanks so much for picking me up," I said. I jumped in the car to see the beautiful, radiant face of my darling daughter in the back seat. What an angel she was. What a devil I was. I felt terrible. What kind of father could I ever hope to be behaving like this?

"I've actually got another show tonight," I said sheepishly.

"I know. I brought you some water and some snacks. I assumed you haven't eaten anything."

"No. Thank you. What would I do without you?" What would I do without her? And a harsh voice from inside said, "You'll probably find out soon enough if you keep this up."

I went home and slept a fitful, broken, amphetamine laced sleep. I woke up at 4pm, showered, called a taxi, and went back to do it all over again. Music had quickly become a mechanism by which I was justifying partying. It was starting to stress me out as it was gaining more momentum, and my only way of coping was to drink. The drinking led to partying, and the partying could only be justified by pushing the music harder. I was spiraling.

CHAPTER 9

Flash forward to my early sobriety. I had managed over two weeks and the initial physical detox had run its course. Then began the psychological detox which was much more painful and protracted. But I set some boundaries and started to prepare for a tilt at sobriety. My wife never drank in front of me. We cleared the house of booze. I started to take this seriously. I had canceled everything. No gigs. No parties. No socializing. I just needed some time to get on top of my drinking. But I wanted music back in my life. I'd associated music with drinking. The two were one and the same. I'd become so negative about it I wasn't sure whether I could get back on stage. I finally bit the bullet and told the guys I wanted to play. I needed to test myself. Here's the post I wrote on the One Year No Beer Challenge's Private Facebook group. It's brief, but it's telling.

Day 42

"I've got my first gig since going alcohol-free tonight. I'm scared. This is my number one trigger and it's a beautiful warm day, and all my mates are coming, and blah blah, excuses, excuses... I've been fine, but all day I can't shake the desire to drink beer. I just needed to say it out loud so I can remind myself why I'm doing this."

It was six weeks of long arduous days of sobriety before I even attempted to get playing again. I sat in the bathroom after sound check. My fingernails were bitten, torn, rough, exposed to the quick with spots of blood. I nervously pawed my phone in the cubicle frantically punching the screen in a desperate plea to my tribe on the One Year No Beer Facebook page. How was I going to get through this? I was in the recently re-opened iconic music venue, the Espy. It was a scorching hot night and cold crisp glasses of amber ale lined the outdoor areas that faced the sparkling bay, the white caps whipped up by the fresh northerly wind glinting like diamonds in the hot air. Every inch of me pushed towards those glasses. I was attempting to circumvent all my musical rituals over the past decade. The illusions, the temptations, the compulsions all came flooding back so quickly. It was demoralizing that after forty-two days of hard work a simple context could reduce me back to the start of sobriety as if no time had passed at all. This is the trap. It sets itself. A trigger hits you hard. The drug tries to pull you back in. You must not let it. These are the moments when change happens, when change starts to crystalize.

I pushed back the pint poured by the unsuspecting publican. I disappeared to the toilets and asked for help. The response was humbling and so unbelievably fortifying. Ask for help. We all need it sometimes. We fear to ask, but then we hate ourselves when we stumble. It's such a damaging paradox. I put on my big boy pants, went out and ordered a soda water. See, this is the thing. These cravings only last a while. This one, so intense I thought I'd explode only lasted twenty minutes in real time. If I decided to drink, it would have precipitated a bender that would have lasted twelve plus hours, ruined my week and reverberated through my life by perpetuating more desire, more dependence and deepening shame and resentment at my lack of control. What's twenty minutes of discomfort next to that?

I played the show and I stayed alcohol free. It was a big moment for me, and I've never forgotten the feeling. After years of drinking before shows, it was a completely different experience. I had to face my stage fright. I had to sit with the moments when I lost concentration, when I started over thinking, when I made mistakes. This took some time to get used to. But I adapted quickly. I soon realized that performing sober is an enormous buzz, and it's one that is actually diminished rather than enhanced by alcohol. There are so many things in our lives we have convinced ourselves require alcohol to maximize their enjoyment. It is illusory.

After getting myself into such a bad place with drugs and alcohol, I was so elated to finally piece together a string of sober days. I arrived at sober day fifty and was starting to feel a big shift in my sense of self, although ultimately I hadn't shifted my mindset enough for it to stick just yet. Here's what I wrote on the One Year No Beer private group:

Day 50

"This officially marks the longest time without alcohol since I was thirteen years old. That's a scary thought, but I'm not going to dwell on what's happened, all the wasted hours, nights, weeks, years, drunk, high, sick, hung over, coming down, all the stupid conversations, risky behavior, bad decisions, it's all done, gone, let go of. I can't change what's done. I'm not sure I'd want to anyway. Are we not in part the sum of our experiences? If so, all we can do is take charge of our next experiences and not commit to anything based on pure habit or arbitrary reasons. That's a comfort but also a source of power for the future, which is feeling a lot brighter than it has for me in a long time."

Such positivity. It was ultimately a bit naïve. I'd gotten ahead of myself. I was rightly proud. But although I thought these things, I hadn't really tested them. I was white knuckling more than I'd admit, and I hadn't really delved deep into the underlying reasons I was drinking in the first place. I was enjoying being sober at a surface level. I'd lost a few pounds, I was feeling a bit less anxious (not much mind you). I was enjoying saving money and having my weekends back. But change, real deep change, can be initiated by these surface benefits, but it won't stick. It has to come from deeper waters. I discovered this simple truth a mere nineteen days later.

I thought I'd cracked sobriety. I went to a music festival. I had every intention of continuing my sobriety there, although I knew it would be difficult. I went to buy alcohol free beers. I couldn't find any, so I bought full strength beer. That act in itself tells you how committed I really was to sobriety. I arrived at the Meredith pub after a long drive from Melbourne. We went in.

"Want a beer?"

"Um…I, er, sure." I didn't. But I didn't know how to say no.

"Here you go, mate. Here's to a ripper weekend."

We clinked our glasses. I was incredibly uneasy about it. I hadn't drunk in nearly ten weeks and it was by far the longest stretch of abstinence I had had since I was thirteen. Like watching someone else's life through a lens, I picked up the beer, pressed the glass to my lips and drank. The beer hit my tongue and immediately my whole body screamed out, "poison." The fire-laden sensation of ethanol permeated my whole mouth. It was putrid. I nearly gagged. As my taste buds recoiled from the alcohol in horror, the chemical that sparked my bodily panic stations made its way to my brain, which quickly succumbed to the familiar intoxication sensation. The dopamine centers lit up. The chemical I had starved my brain of for the past ten weeks was back. I drank the beer. The disgusting taste a distant memory, a fleeting moment when my sobriety had almost prevailed, before it was washed away in the full tide of plentiful beer.

I lost the will to fight. We arrived at the festival and I drank heavily. I ran into a mate later on after I'd had at least seven or eight beers.

"Hey brother! How are you, man?"

"I'm great dude. All the better for seeing you here," I replied genuinely.

"I'm super excited to see this." The Breeders were about to hit the stage. The mood was electric. So many people were excited to see them.

"Yeah, me too. I think it'll be awesome."

"No doubt. Hey, do you want a pill? I've got some super strong MDMA caps." Decisions. I didn't. What had become of my sobriety? I was drunk. But I could have just kept it to drinking. I could try something new and quit while I'm only moderately behind. I caved.

"Sure. Let's do it. Thanks so much, dude."

We took the caps. They were super strong. I was off my face. I took drugs heavily for the next two nights. For two nights I completely fell back on old habits. I let myself off the hook. I let myself suspend my responsibilities to myself, to my peers, to my new friends, to my family. My dalliance in sobriety could have easily ended here. I had done well after all. Time to get on with normal life and stop struggling against something I don't really want to beat. I contemplated it. But as I awoke on Sunday, my lips cracked and pale, my eyes throbbing with the last remnants of ketamine, cocaine, ecstasy and alcohol from the preceding two days, suddenly I had enough of myself. I was so fed up with this same decades-old cycle of bingeing. I didn't want it anymore. I was mortified. I had to start again. After coming so far, I was back at square one. I felt demoralized and distraught. But I did something that I am immensely proud of. In my disgust at myself, I got on my phone while I was still in my tent, still disoriented from the haze of what I'd been up to, and I signed up to One Year No Beer for the full year. The psychology of that decision was as much about punishing myself as it was about determination. There was a heavy dose of me saying to myself, "Here you go, wise guy. Try doing a year, I dare you." Whatever ultimately caused the decision, I made it, I committed. I felt terrible and I was sick of feeling terrible. I swore to myself then and there: "Don't you ever, ever wake up feeling like this again!" Life is too short for wallowing in problems of my own making. I will never forget waking up after that massive binge following my ten initial weeks of sobriety. It was absolutely horrible, and I never want to know that feeling again. I have not known that feeling since that decisive moment.

So there I was, back at day one. Back under the fallen brick wall of alcohol infused amphetamine abuse. Back to the city we drove, taking back roads to avoid any police drug testing on our way home from the festival. I arrived home and pretended I wasn't feeling as miserable as I was. I tried to engage with my daughter. I tried to engage with my wife. But there was no fuel in the furnace. The only thing that remained of me was a steadily growing panic and dread of work the next day.

Mondays are usually manageable after a massive weekend, as there is usually some remnant of latent amphetamines swimming around your brain after a big bender. Tuesday is another story though. Tuesday is when the world capitulates, when the serotonin is so depleted that you become a mere specter of yourself. A shadow. A nightmare. I arrived at work on the Tuesday and had to help organize a meeting for some quite senior officials. I was a jittery mess and I had already messed up by not doing what my boss expected of me. I was sweaty, anxious, fumbling like crazy. It's not how I envisioned my life. It's not in any way where I wanted to be. The job alone was bad enough, but through this comedown, it was intolerable. But nothing is truly intolerable, and like so many times before, I managed to get through everything with a decent dose of deep breathing in the office bathrooms while I teetered on the verge of full-scale panic. What was so different about this experience was my newfound commitment to remaining sober and not fall into my past patterns of drinking to ease my comedowns from drugs. I weathered the comedown. I didn't drink it away. I just had to ride it out. I knew it would be tough. I knew Christmas, New Year's Eve, office parties were all only days away. I had to stay strong and ride this sucker out.

My first sober Christmas began with the biggest challenge I had yet faced. It was early in my sobriety, but I was at that wonderful phase of real determination. The bender of the weeks prior to it was fresh in my memory. The horror of the comedown was still real and jagged. I played a gig at my friends' Christmas party. This crew likes to party. Hard. I was so nervous. I sat in my car and did a quick meditation to try and calm my nerves. The humidity and thickness of both the air and the atmosphere were making me perspire. My sweat was making me more nervous. My heart raced. How would I survive this? There was no way through this other than to just get in there, tackle it head on and do my best. I gathered myself as best I could and entered the bar.

Everyone was already blind drunk. Some people had been out all night from the preceding evening. There was a thick, pungent layer of booze-laden sweat that hung in the air. The smell was overwhelming. One of things that is so noticeable about being sober is how much alcohol smells. It smells downright toxic. Every sense in your nose rings with alarm bells. It is the smell of poison, and it is one of the things that I tried very hard to listen to and acknowledge, as honoring what my body was telling me about the substance seemed to help to change my perception of it.

I lugged my drums through the wall of revelers at the bar, clumsily bumping my way through the throng. I anxiously tumbled my way into the band room feeling all too starkly like the figurative and literal elephant in the room, the self-consciousness that made me gravitate to alcohol in the first place began to occupy all my thoughts.

"Hi mate. Want a drink?"

"No thanks, mate. I'm driving tonight."

"Not even one?"

"Nah. I'll have a Coke though if you're offering." It's these split second decisions that determine the fate of your evening. They are so important. They are the difference between folding and solidifying our sobriety.

"Suit yourself." I tried to concentrate on setting up my instrument. I set up my drums and we fumbled our way through a quick sound check.

We took to the stage only a few minutes later and played one of the most genuinely shambolic sets I've ever been a part of. The band was sideways drunk. My skin crawled. I did my best to keep things on the straight and narrow but it was like watching a car crash in slow motion from the backseat. No amount of me willing otherwise could alter this impending disaster. We crashed. We flailed. It was both chaos and hilarity. Broken strings, whole sections of songs completely forgotten, whatever could go wrong in live performance did. But no one seemed to notice or care. In a way it was easy. Everyone was so drunk by the time I arrived no one hassled me to drink. No one really noticed how much of a shambles we were on stage either. It was highly entertaining. Sometimes entertainment trumps exceptional playing. This was one of the most memorable gigs I've been a part of. I look back on it very fondly.

Despite my initial trepidation, I had a really good night. I think I had a contact high. By the time people were starting to talk complete nonsense, I drove myself home. I jumped on Facebook the following morning and saw all kinds of incriminating photos of them all still partying at 8am. I just thought, "thank goodness that's not me today, as it has been many times before." So, so many times that was me, raging all night and all day. My days of that were done. They just had to be. There comes a time in life were the dissonance between what we really want and how we behave start causing us more pain than abstaining from the things we think we desire. I had fun partying sober with that crew. Some mates are still real mates, even when they're smashing it and I'm not. It made me feel much better about being sober for longer. It was a small victory. The war is won by amassing lots of small victories. Sobriety is very much the continuous collection of tiny, almost imperceptible wins. This was one of them.

I awoke early after that gig and although I was exhausted from only having a few hours sleep, I was really proud of myself for not drinking. I did not take drugs (I was offered the works too). I had another gig the following night. I felt fresh and ready to perform again. I also played so much better over those few nights because I was completely sober. What's more, I got myself through that whole weekend of shows unscathed. I was ready to head to my parents' Christmas party with a clear (albeit tired) head unlike previous years where, under the same circumstances, I would have gone hung over, bailed and said I had gastro, or more likely gone still high, still drunk having not slept smelling like an oil refinery and being a genuine fire hazard to the surrounding suburbs.

I know lots of people struggle with alcohol and drugs around Christmas and the holiday periods. It's quite a tense time of year and families can be huge triggers as well as sources of support. Celebrate the little victories and try and let the negative self-talk pass you by, it has no more claim on your reality than any other thoughts.

During Christmas the dream of moderate drinking abounds, as we are confronted by events that on the surface seem to offer wholesome, festive alcohol consumption. Work Christmas parties, family events, school breakups, whatever they may be, the allure of a few drinks entices us all. But the festive season for many of us is laced with the ghosts of drunken Christmases past. I've certainly had my share of holiday periods dripping in debauchery, where the word "holiday" meant an excuse to obliterate myself. Christmas Eves spent in dive bars playing music followed by toilet cubicles where I drunkenly stuffed whatever stimulant I could find up my nose, partying recklessly into what should be enjoyable family time. Christmas Day lunches where I had to scrape the tattered remnants of my shriveled, serotonin-sapped consciousness off the cold tiles of my bathroom floor, my place of rest as the festive season finally began to show its teeth. Family lunches so hung over I had to spew out of the taxi car door on the way over to my parents' house, a train wreck in real time, only to arrive and get drunk all over again. A deeper trench from which to extricate myself with stronger booze, stronger drugs.

This is the reality behind the promise of moderate Christmas drinking for many of us. It is the specter of benders, of a loss of control, of the addict animal within being loosed yet again. One particular Christmas Eve when I was twenty, my friend threw an impromptu gathering at their house. It was a really sweet set up and we all began the night with a few beers, as we so often did. It was a hot night. We had our swimming gear on. The sounds of beer bottles opening, bodies splashing, laughter, yells, howls filled the suburban summer night. Beers flowed. Ideas began to circulate.

"Hey mate, I've got a bag. Do you want some?"

"I'd better not. I've got lunch with my family tomorrow and I'd really like to keep myself nice for them."

"So do I. You'll be fine."

"Nah, I'd better not."

"Suit yourself." More beers. Longing. Thirst. The suppression of sense. I caved.

"Hey mate, can I take you up on your offer now?"

"Yeah mate. No probs."

White powder spilt onto a fake china plate. An old library card crushed the remnants of any crystals that remained. Two large lines were carved from the mound. Notes were rolled tight, inserted into nostrils, breathed through, blood flowed, pain hit our nasal cavities, my nose bled, tiny shards made even tinier cuts, the small wounds that added up over a lifetime of debauchery. Within moments, I was high. All bets were off. We swam. We talked rubbish. Who knows what we chattered about incessantly into the night? The sun was making its first stirrings beyond the horizon. My jaw was clenched into the weird shapes of altered brain chemistry.

"Hey mate? Can I have another line?" Why? It was nearly sunrise. I had to be at my family lunch. Why? Because the thought of not feeling like this any more filled me with sadness. But lurking in the shadows behind this hedonistic desire to always feel this content and serene, was a far darker and harsher feeling. I was already berating myself for getting high in the first place. There is never a drug experience without turmoil, without this conflict, it is the hole in which we suffocate.

"Yeah, of course, mate." More lines. Before I knew it, the sun was high in the sky and the new day had well and truly dawned.

"Buddy, you're going to struggle today. Here, take this with you. It'll help you stay awake through lunch." I am passed a small bag with speed in it.

"Thank you. You're a lifesaver." I called a cab. It was mid morning on Christmas day. I was high. I hadn't slept. I was due for lunch in an hour and a half.

I got home. My housemate was already long gone. I showered. I attempted to scrub the dirt from my soul, which was as ever, a fruitless task. I couldn't undo the poor decisions. It was just a matter of damage control. I put on some clean, nice clothes, the perfect disguise for a person whose internal situation was so far from this well kempt fake exterior. My conscience was starting to tell me how bad a person I was. Shame. Regret. Guilt. Comedown. Hangover. I did a small line to keep me up, to keep me awake, to keep my brain working. This was the thought process. I needed this to cope, to survive, to pull off an event without drawing attention to my reality. The reality was a bit less easily justified. I was doing this in part because I didn't want to not be high. I didn't want to come down. I love my family. I couldn't and wouldn't want to ever miss Christmas. I would get through this event, and then I'd collapse in a heap. But would I? I had drugs in my pocket. I entered my parents' place. I was doing okay.

"Merry Christmas, so lovely to see you." My mother. She deserved so much better than this.

"Hi mum." Croaky, but okay. Chewing people's ears off all night leaves your voice pretty hoarse.

"Come through, everyone's here."

I walked in. High. Drunk. I was out of my depth. What was I doing? I found my sister and told her a convenient half-truth that I'd had a massive night and if I start saying weird stuff to kick me under the table. She laughed in the kind of way you laugh at a slightly naughty and annoying puppy who still needs to be properly trained before people really can love it. I greeted everyone and put my presents under the tree. I found dad. "Greetings," he said, in his usual joking austerity.

"How are you?"

"I'm good," I said in a false display of slightly overplayed bravado. "Where's the wine?"

"It's in the back room. Help yourself."

I helped myself to a large glass of white wine. I made sure everyone present had one. I drank mine too fast, as always. I got my dad talking politics. I love discussions with him. I love discussions with all of my family. They are all beyond smart. They are all interesting, passionate, wordy, and completely unafraid of a good intellectual argument regardless of the occasion. I did my best to pour the drinks and get the arguments flowing. This was both a survival tactic, and what I loved to be a part of in a family gathering. But I was heavily compromised, and my usual ability to talk adroitly about all manners of topics was being heavily impinged upon by the alcohol and amphetamines coursing through my brain cells. I was fumbling. I was sleep deprived and starting to say some strange things. I got a kick under the table from my sister. I retreated to the kitchen and helped prepare some food.

I came back into the dining room and freshened everyone's drink. I was running out of steam. I excused myself and went upstairs to my old bathroom. I poured a large line from my bag of goodies onto the bench, crushed it up crudely with a card and snorted it deeply into my nose. It was larger than I expected, and I was already rushing. I shook my head in disgust as the fume-laden, plastic taste trickled down the back of my nasal cavity and onto the back of my tongue. I gagged. I recoiled in utter disgust. I swallowed and the poison was already working its magic, casting its thin veneer spell over my glassy eyes. My pupils dilated. My jaw clenched. I flushed the toilet. What pretense. I re-entered the lunch. I was now completely sideways. I had no appetite and forced some of the beautiful food presented to me down with difficulty. Amphetamines absolutely destroy your appetite and your ability to eat. Not so with the consumption of alcohol. I drank, and tried as best I could to get my family drunk to hide my shame, to make me less embarrassed about this sorry state I'd inflicted on them.

This is the reality for many of us who have pushed drugs and booze too far. It's not necessarily lost jobs, massive debt, jail, and estrangement from our loved ones. Sometimes it's just a long list of times we weren't our true selves. A long list of times where we disrespected what we had in life. A long list of relatively mundane day-to-day occurrences that were not treated with the sanctity they deserve. Time with family is something I cherish. I feel like although I never did anything overtly horrible, my inability to do the right thing by them by letting my clandestine nightclub existence spill over the edges into my wonderful family's world is something I massively regret. It wasted time with them. We don't get the people we love in life forever. They come and go all too quickly. Life is finite. Time is finite. I wish I didn't waste so much of it. But it wasn't too late. We can choose to start living differently at any time.

I left my parents' Christmas lunch even higher and drunker than when I went. I was going to go fall in a heap. I did not. There are always more parties. With a bag in my pocket, I set off in search for them. I didn't want to miss out. I spent all that night and all the next day partying.

One of the most difficult feelings in sobriety is the fear of missing out. That we are somehow on the bench of a game we desperately want to be a part of. A game that feels like every single person in the world is playing in...except for us. I know it's hard to feel we are missing out. But how much better is missing out on that unquenchable longing that addiction triggers when we indulge in our poison of choice? Those feelings of missing out at this difficult time of year we call the festive season do pass quite quickly if we let them. They are replaced by a sense of pride and a sense of achievement. Not drinking is really hard. For some of us, it might be the hardest thing we ever do. But most things in life that are hard are also intensely rewarding. As much as it might feel like we can't get through this period without alcohol, we can. We're all capable.

To those starting out in their sobriety, you will feel like you're failing. You'll feel unworthy of your friends, of your families, of your support groups, whichever people you're with. We feel all of this because we feel like we have failed at life. We have failed to keep alcohol from getting to us. But there are heaps of us in the same boat. You'll never be alone in this. There are groups all over the world that you can reach out to for help. Alcohol dependence, drinking problems of all shapes and sizes affect more people than you might think. Don't let the drug isolate you. I think we need to retire the self-flagellation and the negativity about ourselves. My life has been (and continues to be in so many ways) a complete shambles. But it's mine and I love it, finally. Clearing out the drugs and booze has not been a panacea to all life's woes, but at least I have a clearer understanding of who I am and can work with what I've got rather than constantly kicking against myself and going into spirals when I fail to live up to impossible expectations.

CHAPTER 10

One week after my first sober Christmas in many years, I achieved my first sober New Year's Eve since I was thirteen. I went to a dinner party with some really close friends. It was the first time I told anyone other than my wife that I have an issue with alcohol and that I was trying to give it up. I arrived with some alcohol-free beers.

"What are they for, mate?"

"I'm still not drinking."

"Still? It's been forever."

"Well, not really. I kind of had a little two day bender a few weeks ago."

"Right."

"Yeah, it wasn't good. I really fell back into my old habits."

"Oh well, mate. No pressure here. You do what you like."

"Thanks mate. I appreciate that. I'm not trying to be a killjoy or anything, and no judgment on anyone else. I just can't keep going like I have been. I got in real trouble last year."

"Really? I never would have known."

"It's a bit like that. I probably didn't look much different from the outside. But I was suffering some pretty bad anxiety, and I was drinking and partying way more than I should. I can't do it anymore."

"All good, mate. We've got your back." We had a great time and no one cared. It felt great to say I have a problem with booze out in the open.

I had learnt a valuable lesson from my slip up a few weeks before. There was another party of really close friends going on. I was getting messages all night to go. As much as I wanted to go and get messed up with them all, I fought the urge and went home. I awoke in the early morning and they were all still up drinking and smashing drugs. That would have been me if I'd gone. Rather than test my willpower, I just declined and made sure I wasn't there. After some stellar advice from a friend from One Year No Beer I thought it's just too early for me to be in that scene. I put my health and my family first and just removed myself from temptation. I had massive FOMO (Fear of Missing Out), but honestly, I never want to bring in a new year, or any other day, in that state ever again. FOMO passes in a small window but the spiral of addiction has ramifications that echo through our entire lives with disastrous outcomes.

As I struggled through my early weeks and months of sobriety, those small victories began to add up and I started to venture further out of my comfort zone. My band's bass player was living in Canada at that time. He fell in love with a girl from Quebec and moved there from Melbourne. He was back in town for a few weeks and so we were lucky enough to play some shows with him. He and I are really close, but we absolutely smashed booze on our last tours in 2018. He'd also been trying to stay away from the booze since then, so he was really respectful about what I was doing. We're great mates regardless of alcohol. That particular night though he and one of his mates from the country decided to tie one on, and I was so unbelievably tempted. They didn't encourage me, they even ordered me soda waters, but the environment, the great show and just the force of habit made it really hard. To make matters worse, I was handed two Dexies before we went on stage. I promptly said no. The old me would have been drunk enough to think swallowing them right before a show would have been a wonderful idea. In the car on the way home, I started thinking about all the crazy times I'd had on tour with my mate and wondered if that's it for me, or whether I would just finish my year of no beer and fall back into the scene and all its vices.

When we were finishing off our first tour of Europe, we met up with some mates of ours in Berlin. They were kind enough to drop off some speed for us. There was a small canister for each of the four of us, but our front man never did drugs or drank alcohol at all. I graciously accepted his share on his behalf. We were all pretty tired by this point of the tour. It had been a long, hard slog with extremely long drives and more shows than we'd ever done back to back. I'd drunk alcohol every single night, every single show, every day. I was physically starting to feel the strain of it all. I thought the speed was a Godsend.

"Thanks for this, mate."

"No worries at all."

"Shall we do a line?"

"It'd be rude not to."

We cut up some lines and snorted them. We played another great set to very few people. It was a freezing night in a really rough part of Berlin. I wondered what on Earth we were doing. I wondered how desperate I'd become. I was doing speed in a dive bar before hitting the stage, playing to ten people. This was less the rock and roll vision I'd imagined and more the desperate vision of a junkie trying to keep it together, an addict trying vainly to keep the party alive. Berlin is always partying though. We finished our gig, found some friends and drank until sunrise.

There were two more shows left. I was now suffering from alcohol, fatigue and coming down from speed. We still had plenty of speed left, and I had a little line in the morning to get going. We arrived at the next venue after another crazy drive through the winding Austrian backcountry. I had done a massive drive the day before so I sat in the backseat and immersed myself in an audiobook of Lord of the Rings, some nerdy solace in the rock and roll madness. We came to our second last stop on this first tour. My bass player and I were struggling hard.

"I don't think I can drink tonight," he said.

"No, I think I'm done too, buddy," I replied.

"Last night, and that drive…I'm cooked."

"Yeah, I'm so wrecked, man. What were we thinking?" At this point, a kid who looked all of sixteen came over with a free tray of schnapps.

"Oh man, I don't think I can," I said.

The kid looked at me and said, "Come on, man, are you in a rock band, or what? Are we partying tonight or what?"

"When you put it like that."

We looked at each other, took the shots and asked for a beer. After our beers, we went to our backstage area, where I poured us out two fat lines.

"We're going to need this, buddy," I said.

"Too right." We did the lines and again partied until 4am.

It began to snow as we arrived into the very last village, a final European present for the last show of our first big tour. It was beautiful to see snow falling. It's not something I'm used to. Large, soft flakes dusted the silent streets of this quaint Austrian town. We waited for the venue to open. Our host was so excited to have us. He poured us beers. We drank them. I was really struggling to hold anything down at this point. I was starting to feel poisoned. I hadn't been able to eat anything all day. I was starting to sweat profusely at the smallest change in temperature. I knew it was my body trying to exorcise the poisons I'd been mercilessly tipping into myself for the past month. I drank some more beers. It was making me feel worse. I felt ill. I went to the bathroom and vomited. I wasn't drunk. I was just sick. But the show must go on. I forced some food down. I set up my drums and the faint excitement of performance began stirring me once again. I had another beer. I had a line of speed. We sound checked and I started getting excited.

"Hey mate. I've still got some gear. Want to have some?"
I said.

"Nah, maybe later." That was a wise reply.

"Okay, let me know."

"Yeah, I've got some left over too," he replied.

"Sweet."

"Alright, actually. Let's just do it. It's the last night."

"It'd be rude not to, right?" I said in a half joking, half fatalistic tone.

We went and cut up two massive lines of speed. We played another show, but the room was packed. It was heaving. Absolutely wasted Austrian twenty-something year olds were dancing up a storm. It was electric. The manic energy of us on stage filled the whole room. It was what you play music for. Except, I was really tiring physically. The damage to my body was starting to express itself. I felt like my arms and legs were on the edge of cramping the entire show. The sweat. It was thick. It felt dense and clammy. It felt like I was sick. I was so self-conscious. We got through. We were all elated that we'd made it and had completed our first big tour. We headed to the bar. We partied and drank with the locals. We did all the drugs we had left. We finally stumbled into bed at about 8am. Yes, the tour was done. But I still had to get home. I still had to meet my wife and one year old in Thailand. I had to find my parent and husband hat again. But the worst thing that was to come was I was going to have to sweat out five days of speed abuse on top of 30 days of the most reckless alcohol abuse I'd committed to that point.

I looked back at this version of myself from my newly sober perspective. I thought of the reality of that drug and booze addled state, the massive depressive holes, the desire to hurt myself in so many ways, the loss of purpose and fear of failure, fear of success, and ultimately, the loss of enjoyment of music, of the band, of pretty much everything. At this fledgling moment of my sobriety I was starting to be able to play out scenarios in my head before they happened. I was starting to be able to stay out of trouble by predicting what would happen and not deluding myself that tonight would be different. This was crucial to lessening any sense I was missing out on anything but pain and suffering. I was starting to believe it. We have to believe that what we miss isn't the party. We can party sober to our heart's content. What we are missing out on is the misery that accompanies partying when we drink and do drugs recklessly.

As I approached my longest stint without consuming alcohol, I was in a strange mood. I reached a point where I was swinging wildly between lamenting the loss of so much time, money, and experience to booze, and feeling really thrilled about the future. A friend of mine, who was doing a stint of not drinking, told me he had recently attended a family party. He was insulted in all kinds of ways I won't repeat here, but you can use your imagination about some rural Australians' possible attitudes to abstinence. It made me realize just how much we have to swim against the social currents by not drinking. It's not easy to follow your own path. By removing ourselves from the treadmills of addiction, or just habit for those less substance dependent than myself, we strangely place ourselves more at odds with those around us than we could predict. This, while scary, is actually an enormous source of pride to me. It doesn't matter whether we're at day one or day one thousand, we've made a decision to wade through the marketing glitz, the inherited wisdom, the ingrained attitudes passed down from antiquity, about this dangerous drug that visibly destroys lives at worst, and at best is still an irritable nuisance that places us on a dangerous slope that only points one way.

As I approached that dreaded day seventy, the point at which I'd fallen spectacularly off the wagon on my last attempt, I began to feel the pride of officially completing the longest time I'd ever gone without drinking since I was in my early teens. It was first thing on Saturday morning and I was about to head to the gym. That in alone was such a change from my drinking days. More often than not I'd be stumbling home at this point, a creeping sense of self-loathing, guilt and exasperation starting to claw its way through the cocktail of stale alcohol and waning amphetamines.

I've never had a massive night without massive regrets. I knew every single time I destroyed myself that it wasn't what I really wanted. From when I first started drinking and taking drugs, right until the point I decided to quit, I always felt that as much as I enjoyed it, it's not my authentic self. The lightness and diffusion of anxiety that alcohol and drugs precipitated always gave way to crippling anxiety and shame when they wore off. That window of enjoyment decreased to such a narrow sliver of time, that even during the window of a good buzz I was already lamenting losing that feeling before it even started to abate. That for me characterized my experience with drugs and alcohol. You do something you hate, and then sting for it when you're not doing it. It's exhausting. It's a waste of time. And time is the ultimate finite resource. It doesn't come and go. It just goes. Forever. It's one-way traffic.

It was at a music festival many years ago when I discovered the decreasing window of enjoyment with drugs. It was a big electronic music festival. My band had played the opening night of the festival. It was such a rush. It was our first big festival. It was also our favorite festival, one that we would attend regardless. We played an amazing set to a heaving dance floor. It's a wild festival where adults go to be reckless kids. It's Peter Pan syndrome en masse. It's a five-day manic party, and at this point, none of us had kids, so we went for the full time and took advantage of every moment to escape our lives. This always took the form of constant alcohol and drugs. After our set on the Friday night, I somehow managed to only drink and avoided all drugs. I was on such a huge high already. I just didn't feel the need. I went to bed relatively early but I was content and happy knowing there were three more days to get sideways. The next night I took LSD. What can you say about a night on LSD? It's insane. It's fun. It's scary. It's insightful. It's pure stupidity. In many ways, it's distilled existence. It's all of life's humor, horror and the uncanny compressed and bended into a full twenty-four hour period. I went to bed scattered, frayed, clinging to the remnants of my sanity. It was the typical experience of psychedelics.

But night three was where I lost it entirely. This day and night involved ecstasy. Ecstasy, the cursed drug I had abused too much. It had a hold on me in a way no other drug ever has. I turned into a wild animal every time I had it. I used to kid myself I didn't, but I now know better than to lie to myself. I know better than to lie to you. I was psychologically addicted to it. I had a pill. The cool waves of euphoria flooded my nervous system. Every thought, every perception, every movement was dripping in the warm ooze of utter contentment. I never wanted it to end. That initial rush wore off. I chased it. I had another pill. But the rush is never quite as good. But I would never stop there. I chased the rush again and had more. Hours passed. Day turned into night. I had consumed eight pills. I bought another ten from some random at the festival. I had more. Night turned back into day. I lost a huge chunk of time as the ten pills had turned into three. I can't remember a whole slab of that morning, but I came to with a pipe in my mouth as I'd just smoked meth. That snapped me out of my ecstasy fog. I was back in the present. What on earth was I doing? I'd just smoked ice with a stranger at a festival where I genuinely couldn't recall the preceding four hours. I got up and went searching for my wife. She was asleep in our van. I found my mates and continued partying until all contents of my pockets were gone. I kept chasing that high. All I found were crippling lows.

So, after seventy days without a drop of booze or a shred of any drugs, I was so thrilled to have pulled myself out of that black hole. We get back our quality time that would have slipped through our fingers. That was what was keeping me going. Momentum. By day seventy-three it was starting to feel like smooth sailing. I felt I had cracked it. But these moments are often abruptly ended by the shocking little fantasies that creep from the subconscious at moments of complacency. At this stage, I had a dream that I posted on the One Year No Beer Facebook group, saying it's all too hard, leaving and just letting alcohol take over my life again. So I posted the following on the private group:

Day 73

Last night I dreamt I gave up and left the group. In the dream, I had a strange internal monologue that went something like, "We all die of something, why not just let that be the way you go? Why all the struggling and striving? Aren't you exhausted?" I dreamt I left the group and cracked a beer. I then thought of all the ridiculous excuses imaginable, twisting, distorting words, rehashing slogans about peace only being achievable by acceptance and somehow using that to justify just letting go and basically give up caring, crack a bottle and just dive into liquid oblivion. I woke up. Thank goodness.

I think this kind of internal chatter I experienced in my dream has been there since I was a child. There's an aspect of my personality that likes the danger. It had relatively benign expressions in surfing, windsurfing, and sport generally. But there's also an aspect of my personality that profoundly distrusts being vulnerable to others. That hates not having all the answers. That detests being out of control. It's the part of me that revels in the self-abasement. There's a long, gnarled root that ties me to alcohol, and it was naive to think that it would have been uprooted in a mere ten weeks. It was incredibly naive. But, those kinds of thought process were starting to last no more than a minute and were quickly being overwhelmed by a flood of positive images, of kind words, of visions of life without alcohol and how much I was enjoying it, seeing how much my sober mates were enjoying it, and I honestly began to think there might be a future without booze. I do worry that I'll have this shadow with me forever, and it would be nice to be rid of it. But I can't drink to get rid of alcohol's hold on me. That makes no sense at all. So I'll try and just keep going and living an alcohol free life. After all, it had only been ten weeks...

I played a gig after eleven weeks of sobriety in a little pub in Fitzroy, a nightlife hotspot in the inner city of Melbourne. It was really busy, and everyone was getting completely sozzled, as is standard on a Friday evening. I played a cracking gig and everyone seemed to love it. My playing was getting so much better since my sobriety. I was starting to feel like the benefits of playing sober were enough to never drink again. But I was still struggling with the pre and post-show situations.

Unlike the week earlier, I was feeling very tempted to drink. I thought about why I was wobbling this particular night after feeling so strong and solid the week before, and it was simply that I felt excluded. It was the first time since before my most recent relapse that I felt like I wanted to drink so I could fit in and stop being the one sober person in the room. That's probably the worst reason I can think of to do something.

"Hey man, great show. Can I buy you a beer?"

"No thanks mate. I'm still off it," I replied.

"Oh. Really?"

"Yeah, really."

"How long are you going to keep up with that?"

"I don't know, to be honest. But I feel better without it."

"Really?"

"Really."

"Suit yourself, dude."

But as much as I felt strong in my convictions, I was sad to be missing out. My mates drank and seemed to have fun. I got more and more anxious. I started to feel self-conscious. I started to feel trapped, awkward, insecure, panicked. So, instead of trying to force myself to get into the party spirit, I just left. Not ideal, as I usually like to hang out with people who've made the effort to come and see me play, but you know what? My sobriety was more important at that moment. In many ways, sobriety is the biggest battle many of us will ever face. It's not going to just miraculously happen without effort and occasional sacrifices. But like all things we battle to achieve, I honestly believe the rewards are worth it. So yes, I had a dud night where I felt as anxious and wobbly as day one. But I didn't cave. I took myself out of the environment that was threatening my sobriety. Instead of drinking, I went home, got up at dawn and went for a run at the precise time when I'd be getting home, my brain slowly dribbling out my ear in the height of my excesses.

Before I knew it, I had reached ninety days of sobriety. Three whole months had passed. After those excruciating first days and weeks, I finally felt I had achieved a significant milestone. Time does move in strange ways. So much of this success, I owed to my emerging support network on the One Year No Beer private Facebook group. I'd been actively posting and immersing myself in that community. It's really important to find your community, your support group, your tribe of people who understand you and your struggles. It is an immense source of strength when we need it most.

My post on that milestone was really a thank you letter to them:

Day 90

> *"I just want to say a massive thank you to all of you. I've tried at various stages over the last ten years to cut down my alcohol and drug consumption. But it's never lasted more than three or four weeks. I never thought I'd be able to last this long. I signed up for the 28-day challenge initially, but seeing all the amazing people on here, and seeing how much damage alcohol was causing to myself and society generally, I am cracking on to 365. To those starting out, stick with it. I was drinking one to two bottles of wine a night and then bingeing on more drinks than I can count on the weekends. Most weekends were spent in a shame spiral of intoxication, sourcing drugs, taking drugs, drinking more, and feeling worse and worse with every passing week. Stay the course. Break the cycle. Thanks to everyone here for bucking society's norms and chasing a better life."*

At this point, the band was still performing. I think we were hanging on to the glory days. I think we all felt the band had run its course and we were back to square one. After all the international shows, USA radio successes and the festival appearances, no one in Australia cared. By the time we'd paused for breath the world had moved on. We were back to playing the dive bars of Melbourne. It felt like we'd lost something. But we still wanted to play. I guess it's all we really knew how to do. Another show rolled around. I was sick. I managed to get myself out of bed after being laid low with tonsillitis. We had a show to do, and in my mind, even the small shows to no one still couldn't be cancelled for anything as menial as illness (oh how this mentality has changed in the post Covid-19 world). I was not well at all and had to have some cold and flu tablets to get myself in a state where I could perform. I felt like being sick was like being a bit drunk, so it was strangely familiar.

Despite my tonsillitis, I managed to perform really well. I took the recommended dose of a medication that has a stimulant, I played well, the tempos were spot on, and crucially: no alcohol passed my lips. In Europe only a year prior, I had swallowed packets of cold and flu tablets when I couldn't find drugs. It resulted in rushy, sloppy performances. But now, I finished the show, packed up and went straight home to rest. What was different? The lack of alcohol. That substance turns me into an animal. I stop caring about my health, about those around me, and I put the party first, always. Once that's happened, I go on the hunt for something stronger. I've done it for twenty years. I know this pattern and I just persisted with it, mostly because I was in denial about the reality of how much it affected my behavior. Not anymore. But not every night out sober is going to be a massive success where we party with abandon, dance sober, date sober, and generally be the poster child for sobriety. Sometimes we just have the little victories that remind us how far we've come. That was my experience on this particular night.

Another aspect of sobriety that started to dawn on me at this point in my story was the lack of desire to do drugs. I had been dabbling in drugs for as long as I'd been drinking alcohol. But I found I had zero desire to consume drugs without booze to loosen my inhibitions. What I discovered about myself is that

I'm actually profoundly sensible in most aspects of life. Drugs scare me to death. Alcohol, as the gatekeeper of my idiocy, was starting to present me with similar feelings of fear. I began to use that fear as my motivation.

So many of the life-threatening situations I've faced all had a common culprit: booze. I couldn't see it at all while I was in it. I was getting some distance, and it was becoming blindingly obvious. For the first time in my life I felt like I didn't want to alter my consciousness at all. Sobriety was offering me more than I thought it ever could. There was a lot still for me to unpack, but at least I had that opportunity.

CHAPTER 11

There are peaks and troughs on the road to sobriety. Just as you start to feel invincible, the wheels come off. It was a few weeks after the three-month mark that I hit a massive hole and started to feel utterly rubbish. I had a moment in the gym around this time where I felt so cripplingly self-conscious I began to feel those depressive thoughts of lack of self-worth and that I was a massive waste of space, a big hole taking up room more deserving for someone else. I didn't want to drink. But the lack of alcohol was forcing me to confront life when it wasn't going well. Depressive thoughts can strike us all at any time. My whole coping strategy up to this point had been to drink away those thoughts. But sobriety was forcing me to sit with them. To sit in them. It can be quite confronting when the initial rose-colored glasses phase of sobriety wears off.

At day 103, I was confronted with the desire to drink yet again. I decided to try something different and write myself a "what if scenario" to interrogate the reality of drinking versus the enticements I was experiencing. It went like this:

So what would it look like if I gave up then and went back to drinking? What if 103 days after my last drink, I decided that sobriety is too hard? No miracle cure for what lurks within, I need inebriation's deathly haze.

"Would you like a wine with dinner?"

"Yes, I would."

"Would you like a beer? It's 5pm."

"Yes. Thank you."

"It's cold out, how about a whiskey?"

"That would be great. Cheers."

"I think we've earned a drink, don't you?"

"Yes, I do."

"Champagne?"

"Please."

Boredom strikes and fear paralyses. Depression's grasp creeps around my neck. Silence permeates the last recesses where laughter once gave life's only solace. The brightness of smiling eyes, now red and bleak, only half open, rolling, unfocused...

I go on through middle age in a fog. Never doing badly but just continuing on in compromise. Small moments where I begin to give way, brought into line by micro cuts, by pressures from the outside, brought to heel under expectation's weight.

"Would you like a beer? It's 5pm."

"Yes. Thank you."

Burdens of desire flicker and die. False contentment rules within. Distraction from fires now long extinguished, no room even to lament their loss.

"Would you like a beer? It's 5pm."

"Yes. Thank you."

Here I smolder, another statistic. But no awareness until the end draws near. Who knows when? Quicker than it would have been, no doubt. Alone, bereft.

Relationships long gone. Respect long gone. Doting eyes perceive too much. Drunken actions etch scars that won't heal. And my daughter's love now replaced by only sympathy for a sick, dying man. Alone, bereft. Respect long gone.

"Would you like a beer? It's 5pm."

"Yes. Thank you." It can't be like this.

At the four month mark, I went to a football match with a friend I used to party with. He'd been sober for five years and we support the same football team. I'd never been to the football without getting on the beers. So I thought this would be a great chance to catch up with a mate who I knew wouldn't be drinking. These safe interactions with sober friends are priceless. They allow us the chance to go into potentially triggering situations with some backup. The game was ordinary, but we spent a good few hours chatting about our pasts, about our recklessness, and the stupidity of our old lives.

"Imagine how many beers we'd have had by now back in the old days?"

"So many. I shudder to think," I answered.

"I'd be completely wrecked by now, and saying a bunch of stupid stuff. Well, more stupid, anyway." We both chuckled.

"You know one of the things I'm loving about this? I have not needed to go to the bathroom once. When I was drinking at the football in the past, I reckon I'd have to use the bathroom at least four or five times in the one match."

"I know. No lining up for beer, then lining up to pee, then lining up for beer again. It looks kind of stupid now, hey?"

"Yeah, very much so. Even though the game is not great, I'm enjoying actually watching it rather than being stuck in lines for beers."

"Sobriety has its benefits."

But most importantly, we talked about all the good things that were happening in our sober lives. It was incredible to hear how well he was going, but it also felt great for me to fill him in on what I'd been up to over the last few months. A lot had happened, and at the same time, nothing much had happened. The idealism of my youth, the desire to affect things at a system level, coupled with an unquenchable hedonism, caused a lot of grief for me, particularly as my drinking came to a head through touring and my failure to recalibrate when I returned. I also lived in complete dissonance: wanting to improve lives on the one hand, and systematically destroying my own on the other. What a strange contradiction.

I spent the first few months of my first sober year retreating inwards. I don't think I've ever really worked on myself without massive amounts of mind-altering substances still having their stale residue on my thoughts and feelings. I couldn't work on myself because I couldn't find myself.

The period of sobriety I'd had to this point, which was still only in its infancy, revealed a fundamental lack of self-awareness. I had started to work to remedy this. So much so I was getting worried I was disappearing into a spiral of self-reflection. Too much self-interrogation could potentially lead me to self-criticism and start the depression spiral, and it very nearly did on a few occasions. However, it also led me to an important realization that by putting my sobriety first, something I'd felt selfish for doing, I was creating a much safer family environment that had the potential to reverberate for generations. My daughter will (hopefully) never know a drunken father. That's rare in Australia.

Some ideas hit society like a tsunami. Their impact is instant and ground shaking. Other ideas are like ocean ripples that make tiny splashes far from land. These travel. They gather momentum. They are fueled by more wind, by gravity, by experience. They gather speed and intensity slowly, away from sight, travelling and growing, gaining power, gaining momentum, until at last they stand tall and break beautifully on society's shores, a full set, a full gang, a full tribe of ripples grown into crashing, earth moving surf. All of this from the smallest change initiated far from the shores of the public sphere.

Our personal struggles, our little battles and victories are the momentum that will lead to huge, earth shaking change. So keep at it, all of you amazing people battling for something, incrementally wrestling back control of your lives. What you're doing may well prove to be more important than you ever thought.

However, alcohol is everywhere. We can't avoid it. I walked down my street. It was a cool, clear autumn evening. There were people out, having wine, having dinner. Looking like they need that drink, the cold liquid catalyst to a stress-free evening, the parched river's drought breaking deluge that washes away the cares and worries of the day. They hungrily poured the drinks into their empty glasses.

Conversations paused as anticipation's grip took hold, the fleeting, darting eyes that betrayed the manic eagerness that you might miss if you didn't know the feeling, the exhilaration of alcohol's first daily kiss. But I walked by, bar after bar, table after table, bottle after bottle, clinking and chiming in the evening air. The bell tolls of a distant memory, a life I hoped was now in the past.

These scenes of surface merriment no longer attracted me. What sorrows do those bottles mask? What pain bubbles behind the nightly ritual? Are they counting drinks? Just one more... better not...work tomorrow...kids to look after...I'd better not... oh, why not...better not... A conversation I had with myself nightly was now quieting. I walked past the bars towards home. I went down it in a straight line, eyes forward, never breaking stride to look back at the revelers at the other end of my street...

Not everyone is going to support you in your efforts to get sober. Many people won't understand. Many people will feel directly threatened by your sobriety. Sometimes it holds up a mirror to other people's drinking. We have to stay true to ourselves in these moments. We have to remember why we're doing it. We're not doing it for others. We're doing it for ourselves, for our lives and for those of our families.

"Hey man, let's go out."

"Sure. I'm keen," I answered.

"Yeah, let's get on it."

"Not for me, buddy. I'm still off it. I'll drive though."

"Come on mate. This is getting ridiculous. How long are you planning on keeping this up?"

"At least a year. But who knows?" I'd given myself a year. I promised myself I'd get through a year, and then I'd reassess.

"A year? Why? It's not like you really have that much of a problem. I drink more than you."

"I didn't feel like I had a handle on my drinking. It was starting to get the better of me. It has done for a long time."

"Well, you've been good at hiding it."

"That may be. But it doesn't change the fact it's been getting the better of me. I don't expect you guys to understand. It's just something I need to do."

"I get that, man. But seriously? Are you in some kind of cult?"

"Maybe." I laughed. "I don't know. If a bunch of people supporting each other to get off the booze is a cult, well, sounds alright, hey?" He laughed.

"Well, don't go drinking the Kool-Aid."

"I think I already have. Oops."

More shows. More situations being thrust back into the world I was trying so hard to escape. We played a show in a genuine beer barn. It was a really fun show. But I left right at the witching hour where things started getting silly. So I wrote it all down when I got home and posted in to the One Year No Beer private Facebook group. It went like this:

"Beers flow. People mill outdoors in the unseasonably warm autumn air. Cigarette smoke hangs thick. The awkward dance

begins. The toddling first steps of people's reasons for drinking, unstable, unsure, newly walking towards nothing in particular, but determined to walk nonetheless.

Reasons? To meet people? To connect? To have fun? Blow off steam? What are these reasons really? I've certainly said them all. How else will I meet someone? I've had a busy week. I need this. I love the band that's playing. Let's get drunk. Searching for connection leads us straight into the grips of a drug that disconnects us from all facets of our existence.

Firstly, it disconnects us from our anxiety and fear. It then disconnects us from our self-consciousness. It then disconnects us from our decision-making faculties, our inhibitions, our cares, our loves, our money, our conscience, our homes, our jobs, our families, our societies, and ultimately, our lives...

The dance builds in fervor. Drinks flow more rapidly, toddler legs replaced by the rapid fluidity of youth. Reasons mix like the sugary drinks tipped into the ethanol cocktails that fuel this cyclone of hormones, of ever-increasing confusion. The pursuit of connection melts under the heat of the drive for more alcohol. The surface excuses now give way to the febrile pursuit of drinking. The truth behind the stories we tell ourselves. Music blurs at the edges, no pauses, no dynamics, just primitive heartbeats in the sickly hot fog of sweat and repressed desires, bubbling to the surface as inhibitions lose their hold. The dance turns into monotonous stumbling. It's now every drowned brain for itself. The desire for connection lies in tatters at the mercy of alcohol's deathly grip. Talking over one another, no room for listening. Loud music. Loud voices. The din becomes overwhelming to anyone with their

*faculties intact. I turn and look at the mess of the offering left
at the feet of the shrine of destruction. I sigh and return home,
but as I drive away, my thoughts turn to a Saturday morning
free of the vestiges of the night before and the smile on my face
widens with gladness... "*

I always used to tell myself I needed alcohol to take the edge
off the world. I felt alcohol made me friendlier, and more able
to cope with the sometimes monotonous cycle of our strange
encapsulated lives. But I've recently realized that alcohol made
me cynical. I used to believe that my cynicism was innate and
that alcohol helped me cope with the failures of my lofty expectations. Alcohol took the edge off me, and the world so I could be
more at peace with both it and myself. How wrong I was. Many
things had changed in the 130 days of sobriety I'd experienced
up to this point. But the biggest change that had dawned on me
was that I had developed an increasingly positive, peaceful and
contemplative view of both myself, and the world in which I
live. I had started to focus on what makes the world wonderful
instead of obsessing on its troubles, on our shortcomings, on my
own failures.

I couldn't help but feel that, far from alcohol smudging the
edges, smoothing out my experience for a less bumpy ride, it
actually sharpened me in a poisonous way, catalyzing a bitter,
sardonic edge to my demeanor. The thing I sought for fun and
excitement ended up leaving a humorless, bitter and lonely figure
in my place. As alcohol increasingly played a hand in eroding
my self-image, this infiltrated my perception of the world. The
internal coldness then mirrored in what I saw and felt in others

and our societies as a whole. I have often heard that the authentic self is suppressed by alcohol. I just thought that was soft new age nonsense. But I honestly think there's no way of knowing what authenticity is if we're constantly drunk. Alcohol takes so much and suppresses so much, how would I ever be able to make a judgment about myself, or anyone, with its fog obscuring my view? Alcohol took away my judgment and replaced it with being judgmental.

So, don't be afraid to reveal your rawest, most private selves, warm in the glow of our longest stints of sobriety, whether that's hours or years. And that, amidst what we might have thought is the chaos of our lives, is a powerful seed of positivity. Regardless of how many days we might have done, I challenge you to experience sobriety for however long you feel comfortable with. To really look for the depth of detail that's available to our senses and emotions without chemically altering our minds. I'm personally very excited by it now, and I'm sure you will be too. It's a way out of a social trap. Clawing our way out might be easy for some, the hardest thing they'll ever do for others, and an ongoing battle for many of us. But out we will get if we want to...

At around day 140, I was away with my parents and then two and a half year old daughter, while my wife was at a music festival with all our friends. I decided I didn't want to be anywhere near a music festival, as that was the last time I fell off the wagon. I thought it was best not to tempt fate. While walking on the beach with my daughter and my mum, I started to come clean about the extent of my drinking and drug taking. I was feeling a new level of confidence in owning my behaviors.

Not shame. Ownership. I told my lovely mum about the tour last year, about drinking bottles of wine by myself, about doing drugs, about losing control of everything. It was hard to say but it felt good and necessary.

"I, um, I got myself into a pretty bad way last year."

"While you were touring?" She replied.

"Yeah, touring kind of cemented it. But I was already heading down that path."

"What kind of bad way are we talking about?"

"I was getting drunk to the point of either being physically sick or falling asleep without really remembering how I got to bed every night."

"Oh my goodness. How could you do that to yourself?" It was a fair question. It's a question I've asked myself at various points in my life. But it was my mum asking the question and I tried my hardest not to get defensive.

"I don't know. But I did. I'm not proud of it. I guess I just need you and dad to know that it was bad. But I'm not going there again. I'm fixing myself."

"You have never needing fixing."

"I'm not so sure. I don't feel like that," I answered, feeling like I was on the verge of breaking down into tears.

"We have never seen anything we were worried about."

"I feel like a complete train wreck. But I know lots of it is psychological. It's been a big upheaval to just remove my oldest and deepest coping strategy."

"Well, dad and I are proud of you. But we always were."

"I need to be proud of myself. I'm sick of living like that. I won't again. That's a promise."

We'd been potty training my daughter, and at the end of the day, my mum said to me that she was blown away with how patient and attentive I was with my daughter.

"You're so good with her, you know."

"I really don't know what I'm doing. I feel like I'm just making it all up as I go along," I replied.

"That's parenting."

She doesn't throw around compliments like this, so I was completely chuffed. No one had ever commented on how good my parenting was before I quit drinking. That was enough to keep me on the straight and narrow. That's why I wanted to stop.

CHAPTER 12

Although I was feeling extremely content with my family life, and my relationships were beginning to strengthen, I was starting to feel the strain of playing music so regularly. I have always loved playing music. But being in pubs, in bars, and around alcohol all the time was starting to wear thin. The cravings sometimes seemed to come out of the blue. They could hit very suddenly, but they almost always came as a reaction to something a bit deeper.

This is what I wrote on the One Year No Beer Private Facebook group after yet another show out in the world of alcohol consumption as a newly sober person:

"Again I venture out into the world of alcohol immersion. Again I feel cut off and weirdly isolated from what the majority of people are there to do. It's a persistent feeling I've had for nearly five months now. It ebbs, then, when I'm feeling good, feeling complacent, it jumps out of the shadows, attempting to lure me back in.

On the way to my gig tonight, I had the overwhelming desire to launch myself face first into a pile of drugs. I just wanted to get really sideways. No particular reason. I just felt like it. I felt like a proper party. But these compulsions don't come out of nowhere completely. I was dreading being back in a pub. I'm really getting sick of it. But something else is stirring too. I'm falling out of love with performing.

I've opened up with myself, those around me, and you lovely people on our Facebook group, a lot these past months. With the questioning of my more egotistical drives, I've found the allure of performance is waning. With the creative and supportive outlets being nurtured in other ways, I'm finding gigs a bit tedious. I used to drink away a significant portion of that tedium and let the alcohol suppress my worries about performing by pandering to my baser desires for cheap, fleeting adoration. With no dampening I think I'm always tempted to fall back on the oldest, most reliable way I know to quiet my mind: booze and drugs."

I'd revealed something to myself: music has and always had, a level of egotism attached to it. Touring was really where the height of my own ego founds its expression. Part of the allure of performing is being able to visibly affect people. I remember discussing this with a musician mate of mine.

"It's all about affecting that one person in the room. I'd rather get straight to that one person and affect them profoundly."

"Yeah, but surely it'd be better to profoundly affect everyone?" I said.

"I don't think it actually matters. If you connect with one person, then chances are you can connect with many more. I don't know, man. I sometimes just make sure I look at the one person in the room. It holds the intensity."

"You're just justifying being a weirdo stalker," I joked.

"You know what I mean."

"Yeah, kind of. You're pretty high though."

"True."

"You do talk a lot of rubbish too."

"Yeah, I do. But still. Make that one person dance. They'll buy your records. They'll get the dance floor going. They'll be the ones bringing their friends to the next gig."

So we got to Europe and I remembered my friend's words. I tried to pick the most likely party starter in the venue and do everything I could as a drummer to make them move, to get them going, to play a private show to them to get others on the train. It's pure ego. It's a little micro game within the performance to bring the audience in with you. It's not art. It's not pure in the slightest. It's demanding attention. It's something I only did when I was drunk. But the nerves of performing and the general realization I was on the other side of the world away from my wife and daughter were starting to make me depressed. I needed these little ego trips to keep going every night.

These people would inevitably be the ones who came and said hello after the show. I then wanted to make sure I represented the band as well as I could and chat with them and drink with them. Again, it's all ego. I'm actually incredibly nervous meeting and socializing with new people. So I'd drink heavily after the show. Each drink would push the nagging voice of conscience that kept intruding on my so-called fun, with thoughts of home, with thoughts of all the important things I was missing, with all the added weight I was piling on my wife, all for the pursuit of this "dream" that wasn't really working. Things were getting in the way of what I originally liked about playing in the first place.

But the compulsions to drink and to take drugs that I felt so strongly that night after nearly five months of sobriety as I drove to my show, those thoughts were starting to pass quickly. This was the difference between me as a drinker and me at 139 days of sobriety. Just because I had thoughts about alcohol didn't mean I was going to drink. I was starting to learn to let thoughts go and never let them take the reins. So while I felt like I had some serious decisions to make about how I spent my time, one thing was for sure, alcohol and drugs only ever eroded that precious time. Alcohol, drugs, partying in that way, all it does is pull time, that most precious and irretrievable commodity, out of your life for good. So I committed to not drinking. I committed to avoiding the self-destruct button. I was learning.

When I was drinking, there were decisive moments that when I look back were the points at which no good was going to come. They were the moments I should have just gone home to bed. Looking at others experiencing this decisive moment was becoming a fascinating experience for me from the outside. I again wrote about it and posted it to the One Year No Beer private Facebook group:

Day 140

The witching hour. The hours of the evening's big decisions. The crucial moments where we leave decisions up to a brain that's had its decision-making faculties disabled. They occur at different times. They escalate in potency with each passing minute.

Now, 140 days since alcohol last wetted my lips, I notice this witching hour hits at about 11:30pm. This is the time at which I notice the slurred speech, the wonky-eyed failure to fully focus, the heavy sweat-laden clumsy movements, the time when my sober eyes perceive it is home time. When I was drinking, this point of the night was extended to 1am. The closing time of many bars in the city. Do we go on? Do we go home? We always went on. Between 1am and 3am when the next bar would shut came the next witching hour. To do drugs or not? More often than not, that decision was now left to a brain functioning at half speed but heightened by the allure of chemical enhancements. The pull of drugs at 2am. That's when the real stupidity starts. That's the point where the consequences last for days, and the effects reverberate through a lifetime. I felt the pull. I was handed a pipe and a rock. I walked. I climbed stairs. The heady alcohol blurred my vision, my tipsy frivolity dissolving under the intensity of the pull of what's in my pocket.

I ascended the stairs now equally sure-footed and manic. Into a bathroom stall I went. I quickly smoked the contents of my pocket and for a fleeting brief instant before the chemicals hit my blood, I saw myself as some-one's son, brother, lover, people I care about look at me with worried and anxious eyes, scared of the path I'm daring to walk. The mist of guilt and regret a fleeting prologue to a night of debauchery and insanity until I finally ended up in my bed at 5pm the next day, broke, miserable, and steeling myself for three days of bitter depression where I poured over and over the split second where the witching hour conspired against me. Where the weight of my compulsions got the better of me. So many weekends in the fog of this inebriated mess, uppers and downers fighting for supremacy in the momentary dance of the weekend's hedonism. A fleeting decision that ruined another week, and planted another neural seed I'd need to retire at great pains later in life.

But I was far from this hole. I was at a beachside town with my daughter and my parents on a quiet, still and beautiful Saturday evening, sipping an alcohol free beer, sad about my past, but hopeful of my future, all of our futures.

CHAPTER 13

"Down we roll, down the streets, can we find our forgotten beat? In a trance, at a glance, strangers dance and pose, retreat, retreat from city streets, into bathroom stalls we go, into our noses cocaine flows, stopped caring long ago, who cares, who sees me at my worst, with dreams of the best, long since left, long since left? When did I get so adept? At snorting drugs from a mobile phone, in a dirty urban toilet, drugs hit brain, brain goes dead, dead as the stale thoughts inside my head, passing off as smart, as fun, but into a corner I now have run, where to go from here? Already flying on the ceiling, there's nowhere to go, so I come crashing down, down and

strewn upon the ground, down among some rattled bones, broken in this awful town, the city streets all laced with grime, the remnants of this nightly crime, drinkers tattered, wallet's empty, vomit on the streets now splattered, as sun rise reveals the extent of the damage, I turn for home, the hot north wind blows me on my course, with my awaiting date, my love, my only friend, my buyer's remorse..." – Drew Charles, June, 2019.

At around six months of sobriety, I had an amazing discussion with my wife. We had a wedding to attend that weekend. I was anxious about how I was going to get on sober.

"How are you feeling about the weekend?"

"I think I'm okay. I mean, most people there will be getting pretty wasted. I doubt they'll notice or care if I'm not," I replied.

"No, I doubt they will."

"I guess I'm still anxious though. It is a party crew, and they only really know me as a party animal too. It's more in my head than in reality though. I think in reality people are far less concerned with other people's actions."

"Yeah, true. But I'll be there if you need me. And you can always just leave."

"Definitely. That's one of the nice things about being sober. I can always drive myself home."

"Well, make sure you leave the minute you get uncomfortable."

"I will. Thanks, darling."

We kept talking and I said to her that the further I got away from drugs and alcohol, and the less defensive and touchy I became about my past, the more I realized I had a serious problem.

"I didn't realize just how bad it had gotten, you know. It's so hard to see it when you're in it. Especially when lots of our mates are doing the same thing," I said.

"Yeah, but a lot of those people don't have kids. We've got a little person to look after.'"

"I guess it's all well and good to do that to yourself, but I definitely agree that it's harder to justify when there's those innocent eyes looking at us. It's the worst feeling in the world being completely wasted and having her look at you," I said.

"I can only imagine."

"I know there's a spectrum of addiction and I was still functioning fine on the surface. I probably could have functioned like that as long as my body held up. But I'm okay to admit now that I had real problems. It was going to kill me one way or another eventually," I said.

"You seem so much happier and more relaxed since you stopped. It might have looked like you were fine on the outside. But I could see you weren't. I certainly can see the massive change in you since you stopped," she said.

I winced. It still hurt to think that my behavior had impacted my wife and daughter adversely.

"Well, I'm never going back to that. So you don't need to worry."

"I never worry about you anymore." That was such a relief to hear.

I kept talking and things came flooding out. I told her about the time I did MDMA, vomited, did more, vomited, until I'd consumed the whole bag and was vomiting blood. Where it all almost ended...

On paper, this night doesn't seem like it was a brush with death. I remember it, all too clearly, oddly. But what it represented was pure self-destruction and the closest I've come to losing it completely. This is ancient history and happened over fifteen years ago, but it had been popping up in my mind lots at that time. Boredom can be a curse.

"So, I went out with my mate who happened to have a lot of stuff on him. We had beers, enough to get a buzz. But it was a quiet night and nothing much was happening. We couldn't find anyone else to party with."

I continued...

"Anyway, we came home to my house. I lived alone, and was single and pretty lonely, in retrospect. My mate pulled out a bag of MDMA, 2 grams in all. Over the next five to eight hours we consumed the entire bag. We poured each other reckless amounts of pure MDMA. Snorted huge lines and lay on my deck in the cold morning air, rushing so intensely I thought my head would burst. It was insane."

"Each line floored us. Like, literally, pinned us to the floor. It was all too much. I vomited. My jaw started chattering, like it was possessed or something. I just had no control over it."

"Did I stop? Nope. I had got the drug out of my system. I went back for more. Same result. I did this same idiotic routine about ten times. By the tenth vomit, there was nothing left, just stomach lining. It was the single stupidest moment of my life."

"Wow. This is crazy. I had no idea." She was genuinely stunned.

"It was before we met. I don't know what was wrong with me. Anyway, I started seeing myself down the end of a long dark tunnel. I heard a tiny shred of my consciousness whisper, "What are you doing?" I started to feel like I was going to black out. Missing moments, as my jaw felt like it was going to break under from its own incessant chattering. I vomited again."

My wife looked visibly shaken.

"My friend left, as I couldn't get away from the toilet, but I was okay and could still talk. I said I'd be fine and he left. My thoughts felt like they were receding from the earth as the hot buzz from my ears emanated around my head and the black hole of my thoughts were finally silenced by a flood of chemical intoxication. I woke up in the bathroom three hours later, there was vomit and blood in the toilet bowl."

"You could have died," she exclaimed.

"Yes. I think I was closer than I ever would have admitted before now. I really tried to suppress this whole episode. I even went out that night and got drunk."

"How?"

"I don't know. Boredom. Worry. Fear of being alone. I dunno."

"But what I do know, is that I saw an aspect of my personality I'm only just coming to grips with now. I can let chemicals become the boss of me. For whatever reason, I can let them dominate if I let my guard down, or if I allow myself to wallow for too long, I am so thankful for my body's reaction to the drug. It got it out of me, and I think that stopped me from having a more severe overdose," I said.

"Yeah. You're so lucky. That's so frightening," she said.

"I did some really reckless things."

"What's really unsettling about this incident looking back now is that I didn't really learn anything from it. I was so sad, sick and remorseful for the following week, that my physical state obscured me from really learning what was underlying that episode, which if I'm honest now, was a fairly deliberate and concerted effort to literally shut my brain down. A mixture of boredom, loneliness and access made drugs seem like the wonderful escape," I said.

"Why on earth would you want to escape? What from?" she exclaimed.

"I don't really know. I have had such a blessed life. I mean, the ultimate escape is death, and I'm certain, no matter how dark I've ever been, that reality was frightening and the last thing I really wanted. I've had so many wonderful nights that, despite being loose as anything, were fun, interesting and really good memories. I mean we have had fun in our lives together. But this night was not that. It was slaving after a chemical and it nearly defeated me completely."

"I'm so glad it didn't," she said, a deep worry coming over her face.

"Me too. It never will again. That's a promise."

"And I believe you."

"Alcohol creates the desire in me for more alcohol and drugs. That's all it offers," I said.

"I know. I've seen it. Not the full extent of most of it. But I've seen it," she responded.

"I guess I know now, at least intellectually, that all alcohol does is create discontent in me. It just sparks want, desire, and yearning for the things that I actually don't want to do anymore. It creates the desire, but that wanting is never quenched, it just changes shape. Once I drink, I just need more booze. Then when the desire doesn't get quenched, which it never does, I need drugs. Then I need more drugs. Then the stupidity ensues. Anxious discontentment, then a tsunami of regret and self-loathing. It's a terrible deal."

"If I'm being completely honest I know deep down I should never touch another drop again in my life. I have a problem with it." I said it. Out loud. I shouldn't ever drink again. That was the truth.

She already knew this. But I said it to her face, while looking into her beautiful eyes, the amazing woman who's brought so much joy to my life, who has loved me for who I am and often despite of who I am. The same loving, tender person that brought our darling daughter into the world, who's loved us both unconditionally and given our fledgling family a caring, tender environment supported by the most steely, strong foundations, of which I am now an integral ingredient, instead of being the source of its constant erosion. It felt like a big turning point for me.

The wedding we were going to I was both dreading and excited about. It was two very special people, and I was so thrilled for them. But at the same time I was scared of what I was going to do there. I was scared of falling off the wagon. I was nervous about partying sober. The whole night was a collection of people that included the wildest party animals I've ever known. I spent all of Thursday and Friday stressing about it. On the night before the wedding, I was in a real hole and feeling incredibly tempted to drink and sabotage myself before I had to face a real challenge. I didn't. Thank goodness.

The wedding was beautiful, wonderfully fun and entertaining. By 11:30pm, the alcohol started to get its grips into proceedings. The stale, slightly rotten odor of beer-soaked beards, red wine-stained teeth, the ever so slight sheen of champagne-laced beads of sweet, hung thick on the faces lighting up the dance floor. Conversations started to ebb under the weight of alcohol's steady, rising flow. It's a funny moment to witness. Conversations shift gear from boisterous gregarious exchanges, to people starting to talk over one another.

By midnight, the drugs were flowing, but I was still having a great time. Then I went to say hi to a mate. He's a chatterbox in all contexts, but he was charging on a pile of cocaine and his voice was an unbroken diatribe of nothing I could recognize as sense. He offered me some. I told him I'm sober now. He said it's a once in a lifetime opportunity to celebrate a marriage. I didn't respond to this other than saying no thanks. He started grilling me: "What's wrong with you, mate?" I started telling him about sailing on the seas of sobriety to the awesomeness of my new life, I waxed poetical with all manner of ludicrous literary allusions to me being a sober warrior legend. I hammed it up massively – well, in my head I did. In reality, I froze. He pulled out his phone, dumped a pile of drugs on it and offered it to me.

"C'mon mate. It's a wedding. When are you ever going to be at their wedding again?"

"Seriously, I don't want it," I replied.

"Mate. Seriously. Stop being such a square. Have the line. I insist."

"Thanks, but why don't you give it to someone else?" I called someone else over.

"Here you go mate, I'm sure you'd like a line," I said.

"Sure," they answered. Crisis averted.

I found the whole exchange really comical, but also a bit sad. Why did my sobriety spark that reaction in him? I don't really know.

I thought to myself how difficult it can be to accept that someone who is sober can be having fun when you're in the thick of smashing drugs and booze. I used to think like that. I wanted to be that sober person, but I was too afraid because I didn't know it could be as great as it actually is. People having a go at your sobriety are often times telling you an awful lot about themselves. Those that feel the need to attack you are doing so because they really don't know what it's like to be in your shoes, and that might scare them. We can scare people. I think sober people are massive rebels. Each one of us has a different vision for a good life, and that may well still include moderate drinking for you. It doesn't for me. I don't think it can. But however we choose to live, by questioning alcohol and taking steps to sideline its power, we are going very much against the grain. It's a rebellious act. Not everyone will support you. Not everyone will understand. But if it's what you really want, you'll be surprised who comes along for the ride with you. By choosing to monitor and control how I reacted to that episode the night of the wedding, I felt like I'd just gained some genuine power for myself.

For me, getting sober was allowing the elements of my personality I had been suppressing some space to breathe. I was starting to feel like I was letting a fuller version of myself out from the shadows. This was and continues to be very scary. I think I drank to fit in, and to alleviate my social anxiety. Without alcohol, I was forced to sit with my anxiety more. But it allowed me to address its causes without just burying it. I can't "un-drink." The years I've spent abusing alcohol cannot be erased. Those neural pathways are there, and no matter how much I'd like to erase the decades of abuse, it simply can't be done. Nor would I really want to. I'm who I am and I had to learn to be comfortable with that. I still do.

But for me the trap is moderation. Moderation, for many of us, is this imaginary state where we can drink without the negative consequences binge drinking causes. It's a tantalizing carrot that promises me the enjoyment of alcohol without the stick of addiction. It's a false promise. It opens the possibility of the addiction winning again after I have shut the gates. Why open them? Even just to peek? I have to stay strong on this. So my new sober identity bears the scars and relics of the events that brought me here. This is not to say my future is held hostage by the past. But I'm not who I was when I started drinking. Thank goodness. But better yet, I'm not the intoxicated, loveable, but ultimately hopeless, reckless, stupid man I inevitably became when I drank. That future, long predicted in the stars of my past behavior, now looks as distant and murky as dark, drunk nights where I've wasted half my life. I'm so excited by a future that doesn't have that in it. But I still have my doubts about sobriety…

Sometimes I worry I'm just gullible. I fell in with a hard-partying crowd and now I'm just falling in with a sober crowd. Sometimes I think I'm just a shocking leech of a person jumping on the next bandwagon that'll have me, after I've sucked up, drained, and squeezed out all remnants of life from the last fad of my misery. But these are just thoughts. I don't need to act on them, believe them, or even overly concern myself with their existence. They come and go like leaves on the breeze. And when they do pass by, as they do quickly now without alcohol, their dissolution leaves a much calmer, happier person. Alcohol caused any little negative self-image, any shred of doubt I had about myself to spiral. It caused my insecurities to exacerbate until I started saying awful things to myself. But one thing I never did, was question why on Earth I kept getting drunk. I said "never again" every time I drank. But I never really asked myself "why did I do that?" I never tried to understand what might have been at the root of my desire to blot out my consciousness. In our sober group, we talk about our whys of sobriety all the time, but unpacking my whys of drinking has been one of the hardest, yet most rewarding aspects of getting sober.

I don't know what I was so scared of. I think alcohol made it okay that I didn't feel I was exceling. I'd put so much pressure on myself to excel. When I started to see that I was not going to reach the heights in music I aspired to, that I wasn't going to in my career either, I think the perfectionist in me took control. The prospect of mediocrity filled me with dread. Alcohol makes just getting by okay. It makes us tolerate bad jobs, bad relationships, and bad health. It tethers us in an intricate web of actions that sustain the myths that trap us. It closes out options by shrinking our world. It's very difficult to imagine new paths in life while we're simultaneously trying to suppress the things we're not happy with. It's almost impossible to see this trap and the way it functions from within it. We need to step outside it to expose it.

This is not to say we can't change things while drinking, as lots of people do. I did. But the elaborate ways in which alcohol supports and reinforces the structures of our unhappiness are more brightly illuminated when our brains no longer crave to be drowned out by drinking. For those people starting their sobriety, it's really important to avoid alcohol. We have to do whatever we have to do to avoid it. Empty the house, cancel nights out, and change what we do. It will get better and easier. But we can't just continue life as usual if we want to change habitual behavior. The upside is that we get our lives back. We get our material lives back, but on a deeper psychological and spiritual level, we reconnect with ourselves because we're not in a constant state of dissonance and suppression. It's wonderful. My advice to anyone in the early stages of sobriety, whether it's your first time, or you've relapsed, or are struggling to get going: dig deep, really deep, draw strength from anyone that supports you. Whether that's family, friends, an AA group, or an online group, lean on those people. They help us in the hardest moments when we're at our most vulnerable and susceptible. We only have to say no a handful of times before we start changing the course of entire lives. The little victories pile up really quickly.

A small thought crept into my mind as I checked my sober app and saw that I had completed 165 sober days. That thought was, "Only 200 days until I can get smashed and have a bender." It was only fleeting, but I'd be lying if there wasn't a small part of me sitting there dormant, biding its time for me to mess up. Biding its time to strike at a moment of complacency. A latent, currently bound and gagged, addict, who will get out and run riot in my brain if I give it half a chance. A drunk little captain, who's been tied to the mast of the ship of my consciousness, the wise crew under his insane dominion finally conspiring to mutiny, preventing the ship, my ship, being strewn on the rocks, broken and battered by the crashing waves. Drowned in the sea of my own ruination.

This drunken lunatic captain has definitely been behind the wheel on plenty of occasions. On the band's second European tour in May 2018, I decided I'd better have a quiet night after a few big drinking sessions very early on in the tour. I'd made the rookie error of partying really hard on the first three nights of tour. I was feeling rough. Already more exhausted than I should have been. I also wasn't sure how I was going to make it through the remaining thirty shows. It was a Sunday. We headed into the Austrian countryside, away from the cities, away from the chaos. I promised myself I wouldn't drink.

"Hey mate, I'm going to have a night off tonight," I said, boldly, to our bass player.

"Sure thing, mate. Probably a good move given the last few nights." We both laughed at this. This is what we thought touring was. Hard drinking was what we had both expected, even wanted, when we were aspiring to be musicians. We thought booze, partying, all of it was just what you did in a rock band.

We arrived at the venue. We set up. We sound checked. The owner came out and greeted us like long lost friends and poured us all generous Austrian beers before we could even say a word. We drank them. We drank more. As we played, the owners and the punters all took it in turns to buy us trays of shots. We took the shots, and played a long, swashbuckling, maniacal set of far too loud music in an old bluestone room. It was wild. We finished our set and I continued to drink.

One by one, the band went to bed. I stayed up with the manager drinking half-liter beers like they were water. We drank. We chatted. We listened to music. We talked rubbish. Finally she went to bed. I chugged my beer and went to my room. On the way there, all the alcohol finally caught up with me. I ran to the toilet and vomited for twenty minutes. I had eaten nothing. I had drunk no water. I had just treated my body like an amusement park with rickety old rides completely unsafe and not in any way fit for the juvenile, hedonistic ride I was subjecting it to. I was sick. I was sick psychologically and physically.

I awoke. My head was pounding. My lips were dry and cracked at the edges. The boys were eating breakfast.

"What happened to you last night?"

"Sheesh. I don't know. I got so drunk and spewed for ages. I'm so sorry you boys had to hear that," I sheepishly said.

"Haha! Living the dream, buddy."

"Yeah, living the dream. Rock and roll. Excuse me while I go and die." Laughter. We laughed it off. I loaded my drums into the van. We set out on the road and did it all again in the next town.

The part of my mind that reveled in that lifestyle I adopted on tour is in there. But I don't actually have to listen to it. I'm choosing again to ignore it today. I will do so again tomorrow. I will continue to ignore it as long as it takes because life is better with that little maniac tied to the mast. I still have a long way to go to eradicate those thoughts, and in all honesty, there's a really good chance there will always be a part of me that wants to get messed up on all the alcohol, on all the drugs. That's why I'm choosing again today to let those thoughts sail off on their own little ship of the damned to career off the edge of the world and speak no more little poisonous whispers in my ear for today...

Starting alcohol free life was brutal. I got the shakes, I mourned for my party life, I railed at myself for being a stupid, weak piece of work who had let alcohol get the better of him. I taunted myself with all kinds of abusive insults that I would never utter towards another human (unless they cut me off in traffic, but that's a whole other set of issues). I wept at the prospect of having to own my issues and actually change because I knew, finally, that I simply had to so as not to lose the people I love most, and for them not to prematurely lose me. Ultimately, we have to steel ourselves against the difficulties of starting and do it any way. We do it anyway. We live. We thrive.

CHAPTER 14

Sobriety is not a cure all. It is not the silver bullet. There are plenty of moments of doubt, of weirdness, of psychic and physical meltdowns, and wobbles and near car crashes. I often became pretty down after having a major wobble. I didn't drink, but the fact that I really wanted to often made me down on myself. I had also started questioning what I was doing and over-thinking every aspect of my life, as I'm prone to do, as we're all prone to do at different times.

I've always been incredibly self-conscious and suffered extremely poor body image since I was a child. I would never take my shirt off at the beach, I'd always wear a wetsuit and I even went out of my way to avoid going to the beach or the pool with my friends so I wouldn't have to take my shirt off in front of them. Boys or girls, it was equally terrifying. I don't really know where this all started. But around fourteen, I became cripplingly self-conscious that I was fat. I saw some footage of me surfing around that age and couldn't believe what I saw on camera. Until then, I was relatively confident. I'd always managed to have really great self-esteem. But from that age on, I began to suffer shocking body image. I thought I was fat. I thought I was ugly. I began the steady self-talk reminding myself I was hideous, had no control, was a freak, was different to all my male friends, would never find a girl who'd actually like me, wished away my youth on the futile dreams of unattainable beauty. Things most teenagers waste their beautiful, precious youth obsessing over.

As I entered late high school, I began working out obsessively. I found an old exercise bike that my parents no longer used. I put it in my bedroom and would do at least an hour on it before bed each night trying to burn off the calories I'd eaten at dinner. I weighed myself every morning and would chastise myself if I was any heavier than the preceding day. I drove my school friends to McDonald's, but I would never eat anything. I'd occasionally buy a diet coke. I was so focused on not being fat. The summer holidays before my last year of high school, I grew about a foot in the period of two months. I was now 6 foot 2 inches, and still eating ridiculously small amounts of food, obsessing over my weight. I became very skinny getting down to 123lbs (56kg) at 6 foot 2. This terrible self-image did start to abate once I finished school. I was still shockingly self-conscious, but I began to eat more, drink more beers, and let myself enjoy things a bit more. It wasn't until I met my wife that I really began to exit out of this painfully self-obsessed body image trap that I'd set for myself. But she'd be the first to say that it still lingers.

Flash forward to my early sobriety, and I again found myself obsessing on all the usual things that I'm starting to realize aren't true and are even less important. After so many years of being down on myself physically, I was starting to see some physical changes from not drinking beer. I'd been working out really hard for six months and it was starting to work. I ditched scales and measurements and started training for health: muscle health (strength), heart and head health (cardio) and, for the first time in my life, for flexibility. I didn't want to obsess about weight and metrics. I'd had bad experiences with that in the past. They're just numbers. They only have the meaning that we attach to them. I didn't want to go down that obsessive road again.

It had taken time: seven months of hard work in the gym combined with alcohol and drug free living to really start caring for myself, and it was at this point that I started to have a bit of pride in myself. My appearance was starting to mirror the sense of pride I was feeling internally at having gone so long without booze and drugs. I rarely skip workouts now, whereas I used to all the time, and the removal of the depressant of alcohol is finally starting to shift how I viewed myself. So, as much as I still wanted to drink at this point, my self-care and self-perception had started being too high a priority to risk undoing it all for the pursuit of false promises of pleasure. And this is the point: it takes time. There is no definite timeline where all this stuff is going to click. It might click for some people over night. It might take others much longer. But going without booze allowed me to have the time I needed to start to shift my self-perception. It's slow. It's a constant work in progress. But some progress beats none, even if sometimes it feels like the pace is glacial.

It's all great when things are going well. But what about when you have a bad day? For many of us, our biggest triggers emerge when we're feeling tired, stressed, stretched, or emotionally exhausted. I had one of those days, so soon after I was feeling so good. It was one of those days where the wheels almost fell off. I hit a brick wall. I had a huge fight with my wife, and my daughter was a complete basket case having multiple meltdowns in public. Frayed nerves, and anxiety rising, I finally felt real, irrational anger bubbling inside. Multiple stresses piled up and the self-destruct button emerged from the thicket of my sub-conscious all shiny and red, a tantalizing promise to press and forget. A true wasted bender was calling. My resolve wavered massively. I thought to myself that I'd had a good run, stuff it. I needed to shut my brain up urgently. Anger turned quickly inward. I felt stupid, ugly, and useless. Why not just go and bury it all in a chemically induced stupor?

I was about to message my mate and ask if he wanted to go get messed up, but instead I messaged my friends in my sober group. I broke the circuit. The reality of the situation was that I had a small tiff with my wife that was easily mended, my daughter was tired, I was tired, and I was putting too much expectation in the wrong places. Anxiety truly got the better of me. But the reality was so far short of the cataclysm I had made in my imagination. The other reality was that I didn't drink when I desperately wanted to. I nearly fell back on the only crutch I've known since I was thirteen. Problems arise and the only response was to drink them away. Problems appear and I'd rely on drugs to bury them. It was always going to take time to learn new ways to cope, and I didn't have all the answers at this point. I still don't, and never will. But I knew I didn't want to drink. I still don't. I chose a different way. Sometimes that's the best we can do.

Along with the string of other firsts, you eventually get to your first sober birthday. My wife, daughter and I went out for dinner together for my thirty-seventh birthday. It was my first sober birthday since I was a teenager. The year before, my wife and I went to the same restaurant for the same occasion. While she was getting ready, I took my daughter to her grandmother's. I got home, chucked on some clothes and knocked back three very loosely poured whiskeys (I always did this before we went out). We got to the restaurant and split a bottle of wine. I then had a few beers and a martini to finish off the meal. We arrived home, and I tucked into a bottle of wine, and then made inroads into another, while she picked up our daughter and put her to bed. No big, wild partying. I wanted a quiet birthday. I wanted a quiet life. But my quiet life was progressively becoming an excuse to drink alone. No one can monitor your drinking when you're by yourself.

Flash forward a year and things had shifted massively. I'd had a recent flat patch and came very close to falling off the wagon in the few days leading up to my birthday. There had been a lot of change and that can be hard to process. Lots of firsts: Christmas, New Years, my wife's fortieth birthday party, Easter, weddings, and now my birthday.

"How do you feel? Another birthday. Another year of life. It's been a big year already," my wife asked.

"I feel so much better. Physically, I feel much fitter. I mean, I'm exercising every day."

"You exercised plenty beforehand," she said.

"True. But it was a battle. I never felt I got any momentum. I never got anywhere with it, so I just maintained. Or stopped the slide backwards maybe. I mean, I can touch my toes now."

"I know. Very impressive." We both chuckled.

"I'm also not having to live through the guilt and shame of parenting drunk, high or hung over on a daily basis. I know I tried to keep all of that stuff away from her. But there are times when, if you're drinking as much as I was…" I paused. "Well, there were times when you couldn't. I don't know. There were times when I couldn't hide."

We ate in hushed silence. But it wasn't the awkward silence of resentment. It was a comfortable silence. I was being honest. Not sugar coating things. Not protecting my wife from things that she doesn't need protecting from. She's way stronger than me anyway. Alcohol made me ashamed. That shame made me secretive. Secrecy, even when it is benign and comes from a place of not wanting to upset the other person, it's still toxic. I was discovering that I was a very honest person when I wasn't wracked with guilt about my own behavior.

The guilt. It was real. I did some things that make me cringe. This was a real rock bottom moment. It went like this:

"I have to go to work. Are you okay?" my wife asked me.

"Yeah, I'm fine."

"What have you taken?"

"I've had Dexies, but I had a few hours of sleep." This was a complete lie. I hadn't slept. What's more, I'd actually swallowed half a tab of LSD when I got home in the morning. I'd forgotten she was working. I don't know why I did it. Just stupidly trying to keep the night alive.

"Okay. Well, call me if you get into trouble."

"Will do. Enjoy work," I said.

I hadn't slept. I'd had a mountain of Dexies. So many I don't know how my heart didn't explode. Plus the LSD was starting to kick in. But I was chasing highs. I cleaned the house guiltily trying to make up for the sorry state I was in. I tried to make some lunch. I burnt my arm on the oven. I was losing the plot. The anxiety was rising. The reality of what I'd ingested started to dawn on me.

What have I done? I began to panic. The walls were melting. My heart was beating so heavily I thought it was only a matter of time before I had a heart attack. I called my sister. I needed help. I couldn't do this. My sister came in.

"Dude, what are you doing?"

"I've lost it. I'm so sorry. I'm such an idiot. I can't believe myself." I was ranting. The panic was overflowing.

"It's okay. Calm down. I'll help. You're okay. Nothing's wrong, no one is hurt." But I had burnt myself quite badly, which I hid from her. These are the lies and half-truths of someone drowning. I tried to slow my breathing, but I couldn't.

"What am doing? I can't do this."

"Go have a shower and try and calm down. I'll be here."

I went to the bathroom and swallowed two tablets of Valium. I got in the shower. I started to calm down. My sister stayed all afternoon, and I eventually calmed down enough to pull myself together.

I lay down, the remnants of amphetamines and LSD circulating wildly across my field of vision. I'd just suffered a full-scale drug induced panic attack where I felt as if I'd finally pushed my psyche of a cliff. I was getting fed up. This was rock bottom. Another one. Again, it all started with one drink, and it ended with me just barely holding on to the shards of my crippled mind.

But as I gained more sober time, and this event drifted into the past, the enormous weight of these trials began to lift and even when the down times hit, as they inevitably do, I felt like I was starting to find other people in the world who understood me and who would be there to remind me of the alternative ways to cope that didn't involve smacking myself in the head with a booze and drug brick.

At just over eight months sober, I began to wonder how I'd ever get past the fleeting pangs of romance about partying. They'd sneak up out of nowhere and I'd be tempted by the images of all the good side of partying. But these were in reality incredibly dangerous, tragic scenarios. How many wild, reckless parties happen before someone doesn't make it through? I really don't want that to happen. I can only control me, so I removed myself from them. But the weight of history and habit looms large and my brain still wants those instant gratifications that seem to have left indelible traces that I will probably carry with me for life. Maybe that's the answer. I'll always have a little piece of me that wants chemical oblivion. But that doesn't mean I have to listen to it, let alone dignify it by acting on it. I have a bunch of stupid thoughts I ignore on an hourly basis. Maybe booze and drugs just become another of those daily lunacies I chuckle about as I turn away and continue my more meaningful pursuits.

I hope so. I feel like by minimizing those romantic delusions as the death rattles of an increasingly irrelevant compulsion, I take the power away from those addictions. So I wanted to do drugs for a moment. But nothing in me has to go make that a reality. No one's holding a gun at my head. So I won't act. I didn't act. Two years after my last drink the compulsion is receding more rapidly than I could have imagined.

CHAPTER 15

*"Fires rage trapped in the confines of dirt crusts.
A molten core burns hot and makes mountains liquid.
Oceans move, pushed by wind, pulled by the moon,
driven by gravity, set to dance on shores of shattered
glass, breaking rock, sculpting stone.*

*In the deep recess of black water, the burning
essence of our planet's soul breaks free and hits the
cold dense liquid oceans. The searing reaction rips
the fabric of the world and begins a cataclysm of cre-
ation. New lands are formed by the alchemy of fire
and water. In much the same way, I feel my sobriety as
a volcanic eruption that hits a suffocating blanket of
the salty water of social being. I love the ocean, and*

feel most at home in it. But its immensity is terrifying, consuming, wild, dangerous and to be respected.

As we unplug our veins from alcohol's drip, we launch ourselves into society's own immensity with the strength and passion, hurt, chaos, volatility and desire of molten lava. We smash into our social ocean with ferocity and pain feeling as though our two elements can't co-habit. Yet...

But as the fire cools and new lands are made, time works its healing hands, soothing our jagged, sharp and precarious rock into the green fields, the teeming hinterlands that spring out of early sobriety's torment.

These early trials are beginning to give way, and the calmer climate of my new world not only beckons from across space, but is visible right there in the immediate horizon with nothing but fleeting passages of time standing in my way. And I soon will stand on a new land's edge with soft grass between my toes and the cleansing breath of the ocean dancing across my face..."

By June 2019, it seemed pretty clear that our band was done. After the whirlwind of touring, travel and chaos of the preceding eighteen months, we were all exhausted. We'd lost something, and we'd started to drift away from each other. This still makes me sad. But like any relationship, the communication breaks down, and you're done for. We'd stopped talking. It was growing increasingly apparent that we were unable to sit down and keep it all together. It's a common thing in music. The love and intensity you share for what you're doing and for each other are precarious. It needs constant attention. It blew over like a house of cards.

I had an offer to play a few gigs with a new band. I had a listen to the tunes and really enjoyed them. It was very different to what I'd been doing. There were more dynamics, it was more chilled, but still with room to go hard on a few songs. It was just what I needed. We had our first show after two rehearsals. It was a really quiet show and I just loved it. No rowdy drunks, no chaos, no egos, just a few nice people appreciating some nice music. It was so refreshing. These people only know me as a sober person. They've never met me with a skin full of beers, a crystal encrusted nose, and an LSD soaked tongue. They've never heard me wax poetical about all the things I have only the most cursory knowledge of. They don't know the guy who'd cancel rehearsals because he was still up charging on Monday after going out on Friday, and they never will.

I enjoyed the music for what it was. I didn't stress about how many people were coming and how our image would suffer if we didn't sell the show out. I was able to just focus on playing drums and immerse myself in some really great new music. Even being in that beer-soaked environment seemed like it had the sting removed. I was starting to feel calmer. Performing sober was starting to be the new normal. I'd finally stepped out of a bubble. I was treating music as a hobby. When I'd removed all the things I'd superimposed on its image, I was left with the simple fact that music is a real joy. It's enough. It doesn't have to be any more than what it is, and I finally felt like I'd let the ego go enough to enjoy it for its own sake.

But there was too much unfinished business with my old band. We met. Finally. We sat face to face with one another for the first time in far too long. Not a gig. Not a rehearsal. A meeting. A meeting to decide our fate. A fate I think we all recognized was inevitable. We were over.

We had recorded a new album in Oregon the week before we'd performed at South by Southwest in 2018. It was a wild, intense experience. I was so proud of what we'd done. Our booking agent, who is also a top producer, had rented this massive house on the Oregon coast west of Portland. We'd somehow managed to record an entire album in seven days. It was so intense. I think it took more out of us than we could have predicted. It was exhausting. We were definitely starting to have real issues internally, but we were too busy and under pressure to waste any time at all. I drank every night. I'd get my parts down and crack a beer straight away.

So we'd written and recorded this full-length album that three out of four of us loved. Unfortunately, the lead singer had fallen out of love with the music we'd made, with the band, and with music in general. When we finally met more than a year after just letting it all drift off, half of us were wondering what on Earth was going on.

"What exactly is bothering you about it?" asked our guitarist.

"I don't know. It's just not vibing," said our singer.

"Is there anything we could do mix wise that could fix it?" I asked, puzzled.

"It's not really a mix thing. I'm just not feeling it."

"But, I remember our first record was like this. It's hard to judge it until we've got a more finished mix," I responded truthfully.

"True. But I just don't know how to fix it. Like, with all the other recordings we've done I knew what to do. I don't with this." I heard the despair and the exasperation in his voice.

I read between the lines here. He was burnt out. He just couldn't see what to do because he was exhausted. Not in the sense of being tired, but his creative drive for the band had been exhausted. I felt sorry for him. But I felt deeply frustrated that a piece of music we'd all poured our hearts into was being extinguished this close to its completion. The desire to drink was rising in me. The same old familiar coping strategy with this mix of personalities was creeping up from behind the bushes of my sub-conscious. Again. Alcohol presented itself in my mind as the only way I could cope with this situation. I wavered and felt down on myself for doing so. But I resisted the urge to order a drink.

We talked for hours going around in the same loop. Eventually, I said, "So, can we agree that we won't put any more work into it. Whatever is there is what we have got to work with. I understand we're all spent, and there's no point trying to fix parts or add any more layers. But, can we also agree that we'll give it to our mix engineer and let him have a go and we can have a listen from there? We don't have to do anything with it. For all intents and purposes the band is on hiatus, or finished, I don't know. But let's not worry about the future. Let's at least finish the work we've already done." I never would have come to as diplomatic conclusion as this if I'd have given in and ordered a beer. I'd have drunk my way through the conversation and then probably just inflamed the tensions, or got angry, or upset and torpedoed the relationships even further. We think alcohol is going to help us cope. But does it ever really help? It might ease our anxiety or tension momentarily, but then we say things we shouldn't, say things we don't really mean, and say things that perhaps don't need to be said in that context.

Everyone agreed with my solution. That was it. In my mind, that was the official end. We still haven't finished that record. Well, it's finished, but shelved. A huge part of my life came to a close. I realized this was going to be as good as we were going to get. I accepted finally that the band I'd hung out a mile for financially, physically and psychologically was done. I left feeling sad but kind of relieved. Most importantly for me at this stage, I'd ridden out that old familiar compulsion to drink. I sat with my feelings about the demise of something I cared so deeply about. I let it wash over me and a strange weight started to lift from my shoulders.

Sometimes we feel strong. Sometimes we feel so robust we can tackle everything with a sober mind. We can go out. We can party. We can take the questions, the criticisms and the awkwardness. We can do it all. Sometimes we can't. Sometimes we just aren't up to it. We have to listen to ourselves in those moments. On a Saturday night at day 218 of my sobriety, I found myself at home. I should have been out. I should have been at my friend's fortieth.

Two hundred and eighteen days before this night I would have fought through tiredness and my internal desire to retreat and force myself into a cab spurned on by a jolt of false confidence, the lure of false promises, a shot of sadness in the form of a handful of drinks so I could cope with a night full of drinks. I'd have gone out with my decision-making faculties already compromised, already suppressed under the petulant whims of alcohol's desire. I'd have gone to this party, gotten smashed by midnight and begun the quest for drugs. With this crew that quest would take a matter of minutes and I'd be in the toilets, snorting some variant of poisonous, life-leaching garbage in the quest for fun, for pressure release, dominated by the fear of missing something incredible that I'd always regret. I've never regretted missing a night out. The regrets all flow the other way.

As much as I felt bad for missing the party that night, there will be more. I just didn't want to be out. Last time I had social-ized with that crew, I found myself justifying a bunch of my life decisions, and I left feeling attacked and embittered. I realized there was nothing personal at all in this. It was just unintentional drunken insensitivity. It happens. But I didn't have to be in it tonight. And this is the reality of life sober or drunk. We miss out on things. But alcohol fools us into thinking we're in the thick of the action when we're losing time with each drink we consume. It's literally disengaging us from what's right there in front of our eyes. So I stayed in and felt bad for a second. I felt like a recluse for a second. I felt like a friendless loser for a second. But seconds pass quickly and the sun will rise on a new day with another a fresh start, another chance to enjoy another morning without regrets of what I had done the night before. A day free of the shackles I'd fixed around my wrists wrought by the simple decision to go out when all I wanted was to stay in.

CHAPTER 16

"Dark Night. Lit streets. Drunk teens. Hailing cabs. Gutter spew. Bar queues. Toilet queues. Sticky floors. Seeping pores. Sickly sweet. Burning heads. Impending dread. Awkward dance. No chance. Next bar. Next venue. Next place. Minds race. Minds slow. Minds blur. Spinning rooms. Terrible tunes. Beers flow. Wine flows. City streets. Bright lights. Head aches. Bottles strewn. Smashed glass. Garbage trucks. Rotten smells. Crowds swell. No rest. Next club. Next pub. Keep up. Drink up. Forget work. Forget him. Forget her. Forget life. For now. Live now. Live how? Tomorrow's problem. What life? Tomorrow's problem. Problems tomorrow. A problem. Problem

starts. Problem ends? Ends when? Ends now." Drew Charles - August, 2019.

By day 220 of sobriety I was feeling down. I was starting to question the whole experience. I'd lost the initial buzz from being sober. As my body and mind had started to adapt to sobriety, I was faced with those inevitable feelings of despondency. The dreaded thought emerged: "Is this as good as it gets?" I realized that I had no idea how my natural mood cycles looked. I'd spent my entire adult life and most of my adolescence getting annihilated at the first sign of a negative emotion. Maybe I naturally got a bit down over winter? Maybe stress and anxiety expressed themselves as sadness? Maybe there's just a cycle of ups and downs that occur in everyone's life and just need to be treated with the same acceptance and inevitability as the Earth rotating round the sun? What did help me at this point was realizing that I now had the chance to learn about these characteristics of my own life. I had a chance to more deeply think and strive for a sense of self that married my thoughts and my intuitions. This takes time though. Reinventions and renegotiations are hard. They take effort. They don't happen immediately. But, by giving up drinking, we're buying back lots of time that would have again gone wasted in a suffocating sea of inebriation and disconnection.

Still, being down is perfectly acceptable, and you will undoubtedly hit bad patches for no apparent reason. I did. As always, I wrote:

Black clouds circle and refuse to break. No rain,
no sun, just heavy gloom in the pitiless sky. As I sit in

the pinnacle of suburban drudgery that is the community pool, watching my daughter learn to swim, I can't help but feel I've achieved a new level of mediocrity.

Flatness has infiltrated every aspect of me. Where once drama flowed and tension mounted, the tepid waters of detached tedium have risen and swamped me. Everything feels like it requires will power. It's running out. What I crave is drama. To set fire to emotions, and obliterate them in a tidal wave of toxicity, to fly off the edge into extremities. It's what I know. It's all I've known. The discomfort of sitting with things and having to just exist through the troughs is making my past emerge like an enticing carrot dangling to again ensnare this donkey. It's all illusion. All trickery. But I'm weak.

Everything I think warps. Is life really better now? Is it actually easier, more meaningful, more valuable? I'm not sure. But I'm unsure of everything. Except one thing. My daughter, the tether from my miserable headspace to the tangible world where I'm needed is flailing about in the warm pools of my suburban nightmare. She is in her element and the joy is palpable. She laughs and smiles and waves and tells everyone I'm her daddy. She says it with a pride of which I am utterly undeserving. But I must be here no matter what I think of myself. That's all I've got today. I said to my wife this evening, "I'm sorry I'm mopey-mc-mope-face at the moment." Her reply without a hint of hesitation was "I'll take that over bender-mc-bender-face any day. I don't have to worry about you anymore." Small victories turn into big victories.

I'd hit a point where I began to question what the point of all of this was. I was feeling miserable and depressed and genuinely wondered if all the benefits of sobriety are illusory. Was I just trying to convince myself life is better to justify sobriety to myself, and anyone who'll listen? Maybe. But when I'm unhappy is when my past comes lumbering up out of the psychological wilderness to try and ensnare me in its traps. That's how addiction works. It's a jerk that tries to kick us when we're down. I wasn't exactly sure what, if anything, was the cause of that low patch, but I learnt some valuable lessons. I thought at this time that I might always default to: "I'm sad, let's get wasted." That thought was omnipresent and how I'd conducted my entire life until that point. But, it was just a thought. It didn't own me. It didn't own my future. I could choose to chuckle to myself and let it pass as thoughts inevitably do. Thoughts can't hold a gun to your head and force you to act.

Secondly, I needed to get a bit tougher with myself. I had let a bunch of stuff slip and I needed to kick myself in the butt and make some effort to get my thinking back on track. That sucked. I hate being wrong, and I hate thinking that I'm responsible for my own misery. But ultimately, I am. So I made a list of all the things I could be doing to look after myself better and started doing them, ticking them off one by one. Every part of my being hates this way of operating, but it beats being glum and it most certainly beats defaulting to alcohol and drugs.

So I made a list of daily tasks. Stretch. Do some yoga. Some static stretches. Whatever you like. Just something that requires some calm, some deep breaths, and gets your body limber. Do some exercise. For me, this meant going to the gym, or going for a run. It doesn't matter what it is. Just get moving. Meditate. This is the hardest for me. I suck at it. But do it. Get an app, or sit in the quiet. Whatever it is, just commit to some time to clear your mind.

That was it. A simple, achievable list. I hate lists. But as much as I hate lists, this really did help. Sometimes doing the things we don't like is where we learn the most. In music it's about practicing what we're not good at. I needed to try and start applying this to living more generally. I still do. This is very much a work in progress. But this is now my default. It's no longer the thoughts of drinking and doing drugs. Now when I'm down, or anxiety hits, as it inevitably does, I fall back on this simple list. It's starting to become habit, and alcohol no longer feels like a default setting.

When we're down, we can't see what we've achieved. A dense fog clouds our histories, a damp veil also covers the brightness of the future, the future being intricately carved by the meticulous struggles of the present. But my past was clearing. As the first eight months of my sobriety approached, I'd been flooded with recollections of how I used to be. How I used to act.

But they were all becoming episodes that were disappearing with time. The fog was clearing. I see snippets of my old life for what they teach me now. I didn't listen to myself often enough. I'm not a wild party animal. I baulked at parties on many occasions. So many nights I'd struggle to get myself out because I felt I should. Because I felt like I'd be letting people down and they wouldn't want me in their lives anymore. I would go out even against my better judgment in order to please others. Everything about me told me what I needed, except my addictions. They were the only voice that screamed for the destructive path. They were the loudest and most convincing voices at the time. But I'm learning to ignore them.

At nearly eight months sober, those voices that called for self-destruction were still there, but they were murmuring pathetic utterances that I can't believe used to be so compelling. There's hope in the futility of our pasts. So much hope if we're patient and allow the quieter, calmer, more reasonable voices their chance to be heard, considered and brought to life through our positive actions. Stay the course. There is no joy in oblivion. Be patient.

I'm not sure I had ever properly conceived of just how potent the paradox of time can be when we don't waste hours of each day in an intoxicated hole. Time stands still sober. Day one feels like an eternity. One day at a time is a necessary dictum because the days feel like an age and we wonder how on Earth we're ever going to see through a week, or a month, let alone a year? Time cripples. And yet, it passes all too quickly. Our children grow up in the blink of an eye, the years of our lives start slipping down age's slope like the early rumblings of an avalanche starting slowly at the peak and descending with growing speed, each increment passing more and more rapidly, careering towards we don't know what at the base of the mountain. But then darkness enfolds us and time stands still again. We upend our lives: quit booze, quit drugs, start running, hit the gym, quit sugar, quit jobs, leave relationships, start relationships, all this change, and it all just stands still. Why won't the change hurry up? Our old ways come creeping out of the shadows at this precise moment, a promise of a way out of the painful need to be patient.

Our lives sometimes shift like a glacier. Even though we make decisions in an instant, the benefits may not be reaped for years. This can be a bitter truth. I know it's at the root of my darkest hours. When I want to throw in the towel because I made all these changes and it's just not happening quick enough. It's not working. I don't instantly have myself together, so why not drink? Why not smash drugs? Patience. If time sometimes moves impossibly slowly, maybe it gives us room to shift our focus and give credence to that which previously flew by in a drunken stupor? I hate standing still. I have no patience, and yet incrementally, the glacier moves, and it is powerful, carving paths through mountains, reshaping and remaking the foundations of my world. It's just going to take time. That is my new challenge: to finally be patient. Good thing I stopped wasting time by getting sideways on every chemical distraction I could source. I've bought back time only to have to learn how to cope when too much of it tempts me with all the ways in which I can waste it. But not today. Not tomorrow. One day at a time.

CHAPTER 17

"I float down a stream, float past the banks of childhood's ease, no cares in the green grass of innocence, we play and dance and love and fight, knowing in the end all things are right, the world is only this green corner of backyard cricket, of tree climbing, of picking fruit from our neighbors' trees, of twisted ankles, scraped knees, the paradise garden of youth's protection...

Floating, the stream winds to the stony banks of adolescence's disruption, smooth stones worn by the quickening tides, mix with the muddy banks, recesses of emergent souls tickle and spike the now flaming currents, lashings of frustrated desires, unrequited love muddies the clear waters of youth's spring...

Grassy reeds give way to a tepid, stagnant pond, barrels of waste pile in the corner of the slowly moving stream, forgotten nights, blurring, pooling, toxic, bubbling fluorescent effluence bakes under the hot summer sun, slipping below the surface, a quiet pond, serene to look at, subterranean poison lurks, life choices, detritus of disappointments, the ferment, erode the pure white sand, erode the smooth, blemish free bedrock, times etched in rings of trees, but far out on the other bank deeper water stirs...

Deeper water, denser, colder, burst from internal springs, strong and pure from deep set stony resilience, passes around the stagnant pool of mid-life's crises, it starts as a trickle, gathering momentum, cleansing the bedrock as its waters surge, rushing past, an irresistible whirlpool sucks all into its powerful center, rushing past reed and stone, past sand and rock, tree and branch, cascading down cliffs, crashing, foaming, a raging torrent, life force strengthens, gathers speed, momentum, and pressure until it explodes from the river into the waiting, immense, loving arms of the salty sea's cool embrace..." Drew Charles - July, 2019.

was getting through my first year of sobriety. Day by day and week by week, the year was starting to pass by. Finally, my dear friend, the bass player from my now dead-in-the-water band, came over for dinner after moving back to Melbourne after living in Canada. We had a lovely evening where both of us remained completely sober. Our chaotic tour spiral seemed in the distant past. The routine that involved arriving at a venue, unloading, setting up with beers, sound checking with beers, playing with beers and shots, partying 'til all hours, somehow stuffing our gear back in the van, passing out or vomiting, waking up the next day, vomiting, tipping our sorry butts into the van, eating grease, vomiting again, rinse and repeat for five weeks straight. I was so happy to see him back in the country and still sober. I think we scared ourselves with how quickly we let alcohol get a hold of us.

We were having dinner and my daughter became frustrated because everyone was talking and she felt left out. She took herself into another room. When I was drinking, I would have thought nothing of this and used it as a chance to pile more wine in. Not this night. While everyone kept talking, I excused myself and went to check up on her.

"Hey darling, are you okay?" I asked in the high pitched, soft voice we use for our children.

"Everybody's talking."

"Oh. Are you sad because we are talking to each other?"

"Yeah. I'm sad. Nobody's talking to me."

"It's okay to be sad, darling. It can be hard to socialize with adults.'"

"Yeah. I want to talk."

"I know, sweetie. But we also have to learn to be patient and wait our turn. It's really hard. So just try your best."

"Okay, daddy." She gave me a quick cuddle, and we played together for a few minutes until she was ready to come back out and resume her mantle as the show stopping party animal that she is.

The intuition of something being not quite right with her would never have made it through alcohol's fog. It would be far too subtle a sensation to even register in my drinking days. I've probably missed so many of these teachable, important moments in her life. But I won't dwell on that. I was there for her that night and I saw proof that every little struggle, every little bit of petulance where I wanted to give up because I wanted to have fun, every little bout of romanticism about my past gets washed away by the small subtle experience of being fully present and available to help my daughter.

I was feeling a bit more robust by this stage and decided to finally go to the football with some of my more heavy-drinking buddies. They're not party animals, but they love a few beers. To this point I had only dared to go to the football with my mate who was six years sober. It was always going to be a test. I used to get absolutely smashed at football matches.

There were 85,000 people at the game. Australian Rules Football is practically a religion in Melbourne. In the part of the stadium we were sitting in there's no alcohol allowed in your seats, so swarms of people pile into these horrid bars inside the stadium. I did not want to be in them. But I was with my drinking buddies. We tipped into this hot, rank, malodorous cesspit of a bar. Crammed in like sardines, the smell was overwhelming. Beer was all over the floor. A bloke carrying four large beers bumped into the guy in front of me, sending beer and glass splattering across the floor. The queues were so long people were buying two drinks at a time, knocking them back in a frenzied mania to get back to the game with enough of a buzz to last them the quarter. The heat and heaviness of the air, and the tight confining space started to flush my cheeks. I felt the panic started to rise. Why on Earth was I here? I excused myself and went back to the game. One mate joined me.

Earlier that night, I was walking to the train and a little voice in my head whispered, "I could really go a beer or two. No one will know. You've done 258 days. Well done, reward yourself." But by this point I had learnt to reach out to my sober buddies and let them know I was wobbling. The best advice I ever got and something I've said to others and to myself is, "play it forward." Visualize exactly what a few beers will end up looking like. It always meant more than one. By the time the second drink is finished, all bets were off and there was a better than fifty percent chance I'd be out all night. Those small words I received, "play it forward," reminded me of my own advice to others. It bolstered my resolve and I held firm in the belief I wouldn't drink.

Seeing the bar at the football after 258 days of sobriety turned out to be its own deterrent. It didn't look relaxing, glamorous, or even remotely enticing. What I saw was an ugly maniacal compulsion, a crazy glint that belied deeper fires of thirst for the momentary, fleeting release of beer. But it turns to a sloppy mess in an instant. It starts its own fires even as it feigns to put out those that drove us to drink in the first place. There is no solace. It is the death of contentment. I left my buddies who may or may not have gone out afterwards. It didn't bother me. I saw a great game of footy and I was tired and ready for bed. I turned for home and arrived knowing I'd made the right choice for the 258th time.

One of my more philosophically minded friends asked a question on Facebook recently: "What have you changed your mind about?" I said, "Alcohol." I then stated that I could no longer kid myself that alcohol improved my enjoyment of any of the things I like to do, and so I set myself the task of finding out if that was true. That's partly true, but it omitted the crucial part about being dependent, about being addicted. But I didn't want to hijack his post with my deep travails in addiction.

The clarity that came from not drowning my brain in booze and drugs gave me the ability to look back at the preceding nine months and honestly appraise whether removing alcohol had reduced my enjoyment of anything. For the most part, it was the opposite. Funnily enough, the only thing I had found I enjoyed less was sitting around with people who were getting drunk. That's it. The rest of my life was infinitely more enjoyable. Even when I wobbled, even when I felt left out, excluded, angry, resentful at myself for being weak and letting drink get the better of me, even in the darkest of thoughts I had, it was nowhere near the pits of despair I found myself in when I drank heavily, and especially when I took drugs heavily. I also found that I could tap into my alcohol and drug consuming mindset so easily because it was my reality for so long. But our pasts aren't our destinies. They shape us, give us contexts, give us scars, but while they can lurk as specters that can cast long shadows they don't own our futures. Start trying as soon as you can. If you need medical supervision, psychological help, group or online help, get it. Find that help and start as soon as possible. Once you start trying, you're already firmly on the path to seize power of your futures from the clutches of the ghosts of the past. That choice is huge, and I for one am immensely proud of anyone willing to take that giant first step.

When I got to day 265 of my sobriety, I began to have small fantasies that I was nearly at a year and could start to look forward to the partying I would do when my year was up. It was a strange mindset given that I was also flirting with the thought that I didn't want to ever drink again. So which thoughts do we listen to? To drink or not drink? Thoughts always pass, if we let them. So I began to think back on what it was like to drink. It was drinking, the non-romantic version. It was the agonizing dance to squeeze in pints between shouts because everyone was drinking too slowly. The three loosely poured straight whiskies I needed to even contemplate going out. The awkward sardine packed queues, my hands fidgeting in my pockets, change rattling, the eclectic beat of the march to drastically shorten my life, the percussive funeral march, somber, anxious, and full of dread. The morning vomits on the side of the road while the poor cab driver trying to make their way in the world listens to the pathetic whimpering of a broken human as the bile splatters and trickles on the pavement. The constant self-chastisement, the empty promises to no one in the dark, still, lonely hours before dawn when I could feel the full weight of my exclusion from the world. The drug-soaked dread that Sunday sunrise always brought upon me as a tidal wave of regret and shame pierced the illusion that I was actually having fun. That was what was starting to be my image of drinking. I was changing my relationship with alcohol.

Perhaps more than anything, I just grew sick of drinking. Sick of feeling ill, sick of the guilt, sick of the lies I told, sick of myself as a drunk, as an unreliable person, because that isn't who I am. It was a poor facsimile of who I really am. Alcohol isn't who we are. It has a hold on many of us, but it isn't us. People who battle substance abuse comprise of a lot of wonderful, intelligent, kind people that are not happy with how alcohol and drugs effect their behavior. I certainly wasn't. By 265 days into sobriety, I could safely say that the most critical lesson I'd learnt was to dissociate the addiction from the person. We want to get ourselves back, I didn't even realize what I'd lost until I started to find small glimpses of myself emanating from the lost corners of my drunken mind. They radiate more with each little victory, as alcohol's dark, hardened mask is slowly chipped away piece by piece.

Sobriety is a hard road. It is incredibly challenging at times. But I don't ever want to feel sick of life. Drugs and booze made me feel sick of living. As hard as it is, there are rewards beckoning for us all. I don't want to lose my life to a beverage. I don't want to miss out on the full beauty of being alive, of perceiving and thinking and enjoying this incredible gift for shallow, fleeting moments of artificial bliss. It is time to reclaim our time.

Friday nights. Once the prologue to protracted debauchery now, more often than not, they are simple, home bound, much like any other night. Am I losing something by removing a special night for chaos? For release? For indulgence? Maybe. I think back to the gentle flutter of my heart at the prospect of the excitement of entering the night. The ever so subtle twist of my stomach as the possibilities of the night flooded my brain, the lure of the urban underground treats, live music, clubs, pubs, strangers' houses, shared cubicles, dilated pupils, raw noses, racing minds, pounding hearts, fog-consumed brains. Futile quests for fun, the perpetual fool's errand. Me, the perpetual fool. Where does it take us, this thirst for indulgence? Through venues, through streets, through bags of drugs until none is left. But there are options in the dark times, the quest awaits, the hunt is on. The texts begin, who is here? Who is out? We get a response, and on and on it goes every weekend, the same results. Not anymore. Sitting at home on a dark and stormy Melbourne Friday night now feels so much better as the memories of the ghosts of weekends pass diminish in my mind. I'm glad I'm here. Here in a home where I can let the growing assurance of my own burgeoning contentment be its own reward without the empty promises of fleeting, illusory fun.

The way we perceive time shifts so much in sobriety. When I first decided to get sober each second felt like an eternity. Those early days of white-knuckle existence drag and drag, seconds on clocks pounding painfully slowly, each click of hands driving punishing blows into my brain. Hours go by, and each one feels like triggers are being thrown at you from all angles. Shaking, sweating, frustrating, until finally the day ends. Those seemingly impossible days start slowly accumulating. We set goals. We hit roadblocks. We hit walls. Day by day. Hour by hour. Second by second, we win little battles. As each day extends our period of sobriety, each day becomes a smaller and smaller percentage of that sobriety giving the illusion of a quickening pace. This is how it goes and why it's achievable. In those early stages, I thought I'd never get through those long days. We buy back so much time, it almost feels too much, and then we start wishing away the time. Until all of a sudden, days start to whizz by and life resumes it's weird bending of time. Those hourly triggers are subsiding, now days, and sometimes weeks go by without them entering into my thoughts. I can only feel like they are losing power and will eventually disappear. If not, that's okay too, because I don't have to listen to them. Thoughts are just that. We can choose what thoughts we listen to and what thoughts we allow to become actions.

My weekends were becoming so different. But I still had to dip back into the booze-saturated world of live music when I was performing. I had another show in the city center. It was September. Spring. Melbourne is party central at that time of year. The football finals are on, the weather is turning for the better and people are starting to go out in full force. I left my home, tired, lethargic, and generally feeling I'd rather stay indoors. Into my car I climbed. As I drove through the bustling streets, my eyelids were heavy, and my heart pulled me homewards as it so often does now. I arrived. I set up my drums. I chatted to an old musician mate of mine who owns the bar, and we shared war stories of touring. It was nice. But my thoughts drifted to the past. Pangs for what once was. Again. Would it ever end? The life on the road still had a kind of pull even though I knew how damaging it was. There's a certain romance in some of it. When you're on tour and it's you and your mates up against the world. And not all nights on tour are terrible.

On our first European tour, we played in a tiny Austrian village. We played in the most beautiful old theatre I had ever seen. We were greeted warmly, as always. We decided to utilize the backstage area and noticed that the room was littered with rock royalty all of whom had played here. Nirvana, Foo Fighters,

The Beasts of Bourbon, just to name a few, had all played on this stage we were about to grace with our microscopic musical presence. I started to get really nervous. I began warming up. Well, warming up or really trying to get miraculously better at my instrument in the two short hours before show time. I drank some beers. I was getting more and more nervous. We were going to play to this huge room to no one. Worrying about things I had no control over was my specialty. So naturally, I began worrying.

"How are you doing, mate?" our bass player asked me.

"I'm petrified," I answered honestly.

"Ah, good. Me too." We laughed. Then kind of winced in anxious pain. The space between set up and show time is killer. I drank more. Finally our man came up and said that everyone was here and we should hit the stage.

"Okay, fellas. I think it's show time."

"Great. Thank you."

"Follow me. I take you in the back entrance," he said in his thick Austrian accent.

He took us to the back entrance and we entered the stage from the cobblestone road. The room was packed. We took up our instruments. The rush of adrenaline and alcohol combined. We launched into our set. People started dancing within the first few bars. It turned out our manager man had sold the show out and was keeping us in the dark as some kind of cruel joke. We played the show of our lives and even did a genuine, unrehearsed encore. We played until we had no more songs. We partied until the last revelers stumbled home and we collapsed in our beds having finally had a small glimpse of success.

Jump forward, and even nine months into my sobriety, I still found that the gap between set up and show time was the most testing time both for my anxiety and my sobriety. This particular night was strange. I didn't know anyone there. It was a show with a new band. We were still feeling each other out. I felt incredibly self-conscious. My cheeks flushed. I stumbled over every single dumb, fumbling word that seeped out of my increasingly witless mouth. I felt the surge of panic. Beers were flowing around me, toxic waterfalls laden with the omnipotent false promises of future bliss, always spiked with the threats of the cold reality of what once was my weekend staple: abandon, insanity, guilt, regret. It would be so easy to quiet the nervous chattering of my racing mind. I just wanted to crawl into a hole. To not be there. To not be. I was on the brink of a panic attack.

I stepped outside. I called my wife. I calmed down. I knew it would pass. I went back in twenty minutes later and stepped on the tiny stage. I immersed myself in my instrument. I forgot the travails of the preceding minutes. I was truly present and engaged in what I was doing. My mood lifted. Panic was replaced by elation. My friends came. I enjoyed their company post show, and I went home feeling so different to how I'd left. It could have so easily been a different tale. It always could be. Our choices have consequences, and as bad as sitting in discomfort was, I was finally learning to let that momentary discomfort, the social awkwardness and anxiety pass. Sit in it. Let it pass. Don't act. It was starting to make me much more content. Small victories win the war eventually. At least, that is my hope.

CHAPTER 18

I t was during September 2019 that I started to seriously consider writing this book. I began by delving into my past and
trying to understand why I'd started drinking in the first place.
This started stirring up some very mixed emotions. I struggled
to see anything but the reflection of my own, painful stupidity
staring starkly back at me across the recesses of memory and the
caverns of time. No childhood trauma. No horrible experiences.
Nothing to blame on anyone else, just the reflection of a pudgy
kid doing stupid stuff with no rhyme or reason. It's a hard fact
to face that I am entirely the instrument of my own trouble. I've
always known it, but I squarely looked at it without the stain
of alcohol anywhere in sight. There was no gloss, no sheen, no
mirage from substances telling me it wasn't really my fault, that

I was justified, going along with the crowd, curious, creative, sensitive. No ruses. No excuses. Just stark acknowledgment.

Confronting this head on was most definitely for the best. I needed to get here, I'm sure of that. But at that moment I just felt like a piece of garbage that I let myself make the decisions I made. I felt little and filled with remorse. I felt lost in the world. But I didn't for long. I bounced back. I guess the lesson I learnt in this was to own your past and own your problems. I had never really fully acknowledged that I was entirely responsible for my own messes. In doing so, I felt like I had finally held myself to account. Once I'd done that, I found it easier to forgive myself and move on. This will not be the case for everyone, and I would never advocate a one size fits all approach. I also discussed a lot of this with a professional psychologist. I personally felt that in owning my own role in all of this, it gave me the strength to realize I could also choose a different future for myself. It just took time.

September here in Melbourne is a big deal. The last Saturday of the month is our football grand final. It's similar to the Super Bowl in the US and it's the city's excuse to indulge in the Australian national sport of binge drinking. It's a great excuse to start drinking in the morning and continue unabated throughout the day. I've certainly partaken in this tradition on many occasions. I even met my wife at a club after attending a grand final party. As I've already described, about forty standard drinks and a bag of MDMA had rendered my form to be less than impressive and she thought I was a complete idiot.

Wild partying in one's youth is one thing, and sketchy memories of the distant past lose their significance over time. However, last year's grand final compared to this year's shows how much can change in a short amount of time if we let it. Last year I had been with One Year No Beer about 10 days. I was on my second reset. My wife was out watching the game, but I decided to stay home with my daughter, as I couldn't face a packed pub sober yet. I watched the game sober. I made it all the way through. I got my daughter safely tucked into bed and then proceeded to reward myself with a whiskey. I then drank nearly the whole bottle until I finally passed out asleep on the couch. I wanted sobriety. But I just didn't know how to do it yet. I hadn't fully committed. A year later I watched the game, ate a ton of cake, and went and played a gig later that evening. I got home feeling energized and refreshed. While most people I know were nursing shocking hangovers on Sunday morning, I got up early and went for a run.

As I ran through the dead urban streets, I reflected on how much had changed in a mere twelve months. Last year's whiskey episode wasn't to be my last reset, that happened later as I've already described, but as I ran I was able to reflect on all the moments where I had avoided my old rituals, my old habits, bouncing passively between come downs, hangovers, drinking sessions, self-loathing, berating myself for another lost night, another lost day, wild chemical highs, deathly pits of chemical deficits, all in the name of fun, all for the price of really living, all for the price of my family's trust, respect, and eventually, their presence in my life. Sometimes I think I'm boring, sometimes I doubt whether this is actually real and I've finally gone insane, but mostly I am experiencing this new alien sensation of contentment. It bursts through the down times and reaffirms why I'm doing this. Why I'll continue to do this.

I was getting somewhere now. I reached 300 days completely alcohol and drug free. After some early resets, falling off
the wagon spectacularly and then resetting again, I had finally
pieced together a solid amount of time sober. Some people hit
sobriety their first time, some take weeks, months, even years
before what works for them clicks. All I know is this: if we stop
trying we are removing even the hope that things will change.
If we try and fail, we at least have skin in the game. We present ourselves the opportunity to succeed. If we give up trying
to pick ourselves up, to dust ourselves off, to strive for those
faint, distant promises of a better, happier, healthier life, then we
are consigning ourselves to the misery that we all too intimately
understand is the only legacy of alcohol. It is bottled misery. It
wasn't always, but that's its end game for me now. It may not be
like that for everyone. But it is for me. And it may well be for
you too. That's really for each person to discover for themselves.
Having a stint of sobriety may well be the only way in which to
discover what power alcohol really has on us.

Three hundred days before this day, I woke up having fallen
face first into more beers than I can count and nose first into
bags and bags of a drug salad. I can't believe how flippantly I
gambled with my life. I made a promise to myself to never feel
like that again. To never put myself so unnecessarily in harm's
way. I took that promise and used it to fire my sobriety, to fully
commit to changing this tired, repetitive narrative, to finally stop
whispering empty promises to the wind only to find myself in
the same old situation the following weekend. Change is really
hard. But it's inevitable. We might as well have a say in which
direction it goes.

But did I really have a problem? Sometimes I wonder if I'm just making it all up. I mean, people clearly drink more than I did and still function. I wasn't ready to hear the extent of my problems with substances when I started. Other people I hung out with were far worse. I didn't really have a problem, did I? It doesn't really matter. If you drink two glasses of wine every night and feel like it's too much, then it's too much. Where we draw the line is just a matter of what helps us sleep at night. It's our own ethics. I could easily justify my consumption. I spent the majority of my life doing just that. But deep down, I knew I did have a problem. Deep down, I've never been comfortable with my alcohol and drug consumption. It's a warped tangle of shame, guilt, wild excess, empty promises, life threatening lunacy, middling tedium and white-knuckle sweats in the deep, dark hours of drug fueled isolation, when the party cleared, when reality crashed in through the dizzying haze of whatever garbage I'd bludgeoned my brain with. This overly dramatic way to live is really not a glamorous one. As much as I've had pangs, as much as I've felt the stabs of jealousy, grief and longing for my past life, the reality is that life is a lot smoother and easier. It's more fun. It's more full.

The life of partying is receding into the foggy recesses of memory. It's passing into the realm of dreams, its significance now takes the form of lessons. Just lessons. About my personality, and about how I can proceed in life in a more meaningful and fulfilling way without falling blindly into my past traps. Time is so precious. I've always felt like I wasted so much of it. But it's not really ever wasted if we learn from it. So I'm choosing to take some valuable lessons from the things I'd probably rather erase. These moments, as much as they make me cringe, are part of who I am. I am starting to feel a lot more comfortable with that person. And I'm sure we can all take valuable instruction from our pasts.

Wrapped up with my conception of partying was the city in which I live. The city itself was fast becoming the representation of my past party life. I've always loved the city, the bustle, the people, the nightlife. It's been something I've been immersed in my whole life. I have never lived outside of a throbbing metropolis. As a musician for most of my adulthood, the city was the heartbeat of creativity. But it also comes with its inherent vices. Melbourne is not the size of London or New York, but it is a city that likes to party. There are many clubs and bars that are open all night. There's always another venue that will serve you booze, any time of day on the weekends. There are clubs you can hit at 5am, find the dodgiest looking guy to whom a sidewise glance the wrong way will result in you getting stabbed, find a way of subtly inquiring about the acquisition of drugs without getting stabbed, and party all day. I have done many walks of shame on Monday morning when the city enticements entirely got the better of me and the weekend was wallowed away in a sea of neon blurry excess and ridiculous jaw tremors punctuating garbage conversations. Such predicaments always started the same way: with one drink, with a decision for "a drink or two somewhere." I never, ever intended to end up at these underground hovels, poorer, sicker, and facing a week of comedown despair. Not once.

The city, the locus of debauchery, the site of some of my most shameful encounters was losing its appeal. What was once exciting was now anxiety-producing. What was once thrilling was now overwhelming. The endless sea of bars and clubs jockeying for my money was now mildly infuriating. This had been a huge change for me over the preceding year. I couldn't handle the noise of the city anymore. The sea, the trees, the quiet, it was calling with calm intensity more and more each day. And on the precipice of abandoning the city, I couldn't help but wonder what would have been if I'd never let go of alcohol. Hopefully, I'll never know the answer to that question.

We look back and what do we see? Messes, plans in tatters, narratives with dead ends, tales half told, roads partially travelled, dreams that remain fantasy, regrets, sorrow, heartache, lost love, poor choices. Our pasts are written. They can't be unwritten. But writing is only a fraction of any story. We are natural storytellers and our brains extrapolate entire mythic epics from squiggles on pages. What's written is never as important as the meaning we derive from interpreting what's there. This takes time. But I'm starting to interpret entirely different meanings from the sketchy scribbling of my own slightly checkered past. The tattered pages stained by the alcohol and amphetamine cocktail that I poured all over the bound journals of my own history. The damage is done. But the lessons are just beginning. So if there's serious learning and growth to be gleaned from the darker moments, then I'm glad those moments existed. I didn't really know what I was getting into when I started getting sober. I just knew I wanted to be a better dad to my daughter. As I get further into it, I'm also doing it for myself, for my wife and my extended family, for my community, and ultimately for society. Being alive is a gift, one that I hope to cherish for many more years.

CHAPTER 19

At my daughter's third birthday party, I was offered some fancy French wine. I was standing with the mother of one of my daughter's best friends. She is a wonderful person and someone I have really enjoyed getting to know. She noticed that I refused the wine and quizzed me.

"Why didn't you take it?" She asked earnestly.

"I don't drink alcohol," I answered in a friendly tone.

"Oh. Really? It's not often you hear that in this country. Particularly men our age."

"No, it's pretty weird," I admitted.

"Do you just not like the taste, or for health reasons?" She asked, trying not to pry.

"No. I liked drinking, a lot actually. You know how I did a lot of touring with my band last year and the year before? Well, I kind of drank myself into a bit of a hole. I had to have a break. So I thought I'd challenge myself to doing a year off it."

"Ah, okay. Do you think you'll drink again when the year is up?"

"To be honest, no. I think I'm done with it. I realize it's really early days, but I feel so much better without it. It's just something I'd rather not be worrying about."

"Fair enough too," she responded. I felt like I didn't have anything to hide. I was happy to answer questions, and not drinking is weird in this country, so I am still always happy to talk about it. Three weeks later at her own daughter's party, she very kindly poured me a mineral water. No questions asked. It was very, very considerate and I so appreciated the gesture.

It's those kinds of small actions that mean so much to us. I felt momentarily included. But I must admit, I watched with a certain amount of envy as the parents, grandparents and relatives all helped themselves to alcoholic drinks. No one got plastered. It was all very moderate. I looked into this picture of normalcy with a real sense of exclusion. I felt like the alcoholic elephant in the room who can't touch a drop for fear of launching into a wild stampede. I felt on the outer and wondered how I'd ever got to this position. When we left the party, I then drove my daughter away from the city to the ocean-side town we were spending our weekends in. As she slept off her sugar high, I thought, "am I really never going to drink again?" I'd said it out loud to someone. I reminisced about all the wild parties and the crazy moments I've had. I thought about what I'm really missing out on.

As I drove the remnants of the city skyline dematerialized in the rear-view mirror making way for the green rolling hills of the pastoral peninsula. A thought kept piercing those romantic images of the "fun" parties. And there were plenty of times when it was fun. The thought that shattered the illusion was that feeling of dread waking up knowing that I'd done it again, that I'd just gone and done it all again. That my week ahead was now going to be infinitely harder, no matter what it held in store. I was going to battle. That I had just done everything again after swearing to myself I wouldn't and couldn't do it again, again and again, like a broken record. That's what I'm really missing out on. Dread. Comedowns. Hundreds, sometimes thousands of dollars that barely touched my account before it flew off into the deep reaches of the black market. Absolute garbage conversations that I can barely remember and would probably be completely mortified by if I could. Precarious, stupid situations. Danger. Mental health issues. Flailing fragments of self-worth whimpering away into nothingness. Empty musings of a frazzled mind on the tail end of the fake happiness of the massive serotonin dumps that punctuated each frivolous weekend. Manipulations of brain chemistry that just scare me to death now. That's really what I'm missing out on, and I'm so thankful I am.

The big day had finally arrived. I had made it to 365 days without alcohol or drugs. Here's what I wrote on the One Year No Beer private Facebook page:

Day 365

I awake. The stale, putrid after taste of cigarettes tarnishes my parched mouth. The throbbing of my temples reverberates, each pulse a sharp jabbing pain, the true remnants of the night's revelry. I cough. Dust and smoke. Heat and fire. A torn throat that is as dry and lifeless as the dust bitten farmland we have been partying in. I unzip my tent and stumble out into the blazing Australian sun. Sweat drips down my forehead. Clammy dew slicks my hands. My stomach churns, groaning in pathetic whimpers. I feel poisoned.

I trace back the two nights before. Friday night. Beers. Many beers. Ecstasy. Cocaine. Ketamine. Sleep at 8am. I awake at midday. I drink my first drink. I've consumed no food, and only some water. My stomach is too knotted from all the amphetamines to consider eating any real food. Yet, somehow more alcohol slips seamlessly down my gullet. By 2pm I'm drunk again. The remnants of chemical enhancements from the night before float around my now booze riddled mind. The familiar swirl of drugs and alcohol begins pressuring my psyche. The hunt resumes with a new intensity. Ecstasy, cocaine, ketamine, LSD, more and more alcohol.

I'm flying again. The rest is a blur. A standard night of giddy hedonism until I finally stumble back to my tent, bloated, full to the gunnels like a sinking ship that's taking on water, floundering under the weight of that which tries to swallow it whole. I finally topple, empty-

ing the contents of my stomach onto a poor unsuspecting shrub before rolling into my tent to sleep off yet another bender I never intended to have.

I woke up from that weekend one year ago today and swore to myself never again. And for once, I really meant it. I knew I meant it, because I didn't tell anyone, other than the wonderful people here who I knew would help keep me accountable. I just said to myself I had to do it by my actions, not by my words. I reset my challenge and upgraded to 365. Initially, I didn't tell my wife, friends and family. I told no one. I needed to act first. I was so fed up. After seventy days of sobriety, one drink was all it took before I plunged headfirst and reckless into the same drug saturated lunacy I've always done. Seventy days of hard fought sobriety melted away like snowflakes in my sweaty palms.

But I did act. I cancelled gigs, I cancelled parties, I pulled out of any social engagement I possibly could in order to try and get a handle on my drinking. I had finally and deeply decided enough was enough. This wasn't a break. This wasn't a brief spell on the sidelines resetting my tolerance, impatiently waiting on the bench before I could jump back on the team and smash booze again. I wanted to change permanently. I was sick of the person I became when I was drunk. Sick of the example I was setting my daughter. Sick of feeling sick. I set about making my thinking and behaviors fall in line with my decision to pursue non-drinking. I read the emails, I got involved in the group, read quit-lit, wrote, exercised, took up new hobbies, kept busy and tried to reinvent sobriety for myself as the desired state, and inebriation as a manifestation of personal hell, which it had become. I began to see clearly what my previous lifestyle really was, and it wasn't good.

My whole philosophy to sobriety has been simply this:

Don't drink alcohol. None. Not a drop. Do anything else, but do not drink. It sounds so self-evident to barely warrant repeating, but it is the best piece of advice I received and it is the best advice I can think of to pass on. Do anything else, eat the cake, have the coffees, eat the cheese, but close the door on alcohol and keep it firmly shut. We do not need alcohol. It is just years of programming, and it can be deprogrammed. No one was ever holding a gun to my head forcing me to drink. Cravings come. Cravings pass. Ultimately, I could decide. But I had to deeply commit, down in the core of my being to not drinking as my goal. Then it was just a matter of sticking to that commitment.

The only way for me to do this was brutal honesty with myself. I told my entire family the extent of my excesses when I was ready. I owned up to all the crazy things I've done when I was ready. I talked as openly as I could here, and with those closest to me. I let vulnerability be the bedrock of my newfound sense of self. It was this openness that caused me some of my worst sadness and crippling anxiety, but ultimately it has liberated me. I finally now feel unencumbered by my past. It's part of me, and I'm totally okay with who I am now. After a year of sobriety, I am starting to feel okay with myself. That is a supreme gift, and something I'll be eternally grateful for. It's the start I needed.

There's a band from Australia who wrote about how healthy living is just how we pass the time in between benders. This was my motto for my entire adolescent and early adult life. I exercised, I studied, I applied myself to sport, to music, but the weekend would come and I would destroy myself. It was a world of extremes that I absolutely reveled in. I thought it made me cool. Made me unique. It actually just made me a bit immature. Occasionally I'd push it too hard and pull my head in. After a particularly epic trip on some seriously strong hallucinogens, I managed three weeks of abstinence, only to throw in the towel on a convenient Friday night and immerse myself into the lugubrious pit of pints, pubs, then clubs, and drugs.

Could I undo the damage on the weekend if I ate well and exercised? I thought I could. I thought I was doing a good job of that. But as the alcohol started to seep in through the frayed seams of the tattered cloak of my happiness, I started to skip the healthy eating, to miss sessions in the gym, to miss out on things. It dawned on me that alcohol was starting to rob me of things I valued, of my values even. It was this realization that made ditching alcohol realistic. We have to replace it with things we've been missing out on. For me, it was exercise, practicing my instrument and writing. I was playing so much music, but barely taking the time to practice and hone my skills. I had completely stopped writing for years, as I was too sideways to even re-read the garbled, scribbled nonsense that tipped out of my booze-soaked brain. If we sit on the sidelines and watch drinkers like envious kids dying to get back in the game, it's only a matter of time before we throw ourselves back into that game and get chewed up and spat out by alcohol all over again. We have to change the game altogether. Create one where there's just no room for alcohol. Where new ways of being take over from old ones. Where we change the script, change the rules, leave it out in the cold like it's done for us more times than any of us would care to count.

We get bogged down in the minutiae of daily life, the boredom, the drudgery, the stress, and the chaos. But pull back for a second and think about the absolute miracle that you are, about the irreplaceable collection of atoms that you are, about your ultimate significance as the eyes through which we collectively know our place. Even more miraculous than your mere existence is the fact that you all, every single one you, are capable of taking control of your consciousness, your divine gift, back from the clutches of a really potent drug that erodes our sense of wonder at ourselves, a drug that erodes our confidence and fills our head with feelings of worthlessness, shame, guilt, and depression. It doesn't matter what day, hour, minute, year, or decade you find yourself on this path to reclaim mastery of our consciousness, the fact you are willing and able to wrestle back control of your divine gift is miraculous. Everyone reading this, however you decide to do it: whether you blip, reset, relapse, moderate, or never drink again. Everyone - absolutely everyone - should be proud of yourselves. We're all on the same team. And we are miracles.

CONCLUSION

had a jacket. Trivial, I know. It's a jacket I bought in a vintage shop in Montreal after I realized my Australian clothing had woefully underprepared me for spring in Quebec. I loved this jacket. It fit perfectly. It was cool. It was warm. I wore it all around Canada, through sleet and rain. Through beer and cigarette smoke-soaked ether. I brought it home with me. I loved it.

I took it on tour to Europe, my favorite piece of tour armor. It went with me through the cobbled streets of Prague, all through the absinthe-laden dungeons of that great city. It was there in press shots, in live videos in strange old eastern bloc buildings that now house the student radio stations that played our music. I wore it through the desperate cold of November nights in the Austrian countryside.

I wore it as the first licks of snow fell on my Australian hair in the outskirts of the Italian Alps. I wore it through countless nightclubs. It parked in many corners of Berlin and Hamburg's seedy drinking holes while I laid waste to my consciousness in a sea of drugs and booze post shows. It was with me in countless toilets as I exhumed the contents of my alcohol-bloated stomach, while I whimpered breathy pleas into the porcelain. Pleas I'd forget short hours later as I repeated the cycle. It went where I went. It became my hardened tour armor.

It came home with me. It has sat in my cupboard ever since. It doesn't fit any more. It no longer gives warmth. It no longer gives solace. It's not my armor. It's the weight of the past, a sensory stimulus that transports me to those nights, those scenes, and those excesses. It's not me anymore.

After glancing at it in my wardrobe for the past year, I finally pulled it out, placed it in a garbage bag and took it to the local secondhand clothes store, dropped it off and turned my back on that part of my life. A small yet symbolic shedding of another piece of a layered mask that had worn out its usefulness. I hopped back in the car with my daughter and wife and drove away from the city towards the coast.

We drove. A straight road lined by thick, sunburnt grass overhung by tall dancing gum trees. Cars everywhere. I turned into the afternoon crush at the rural supermarket.

People flooded in. People came out with their cases of beer slung over their sun-reddened shoulders, with their wines tucked under their arms, their fingers stuck into the thin cardboard holes that house their cans of sickly sweet, caffeinated booze mixers.

I walked into the supermarket. I passed the liquor store that opens enticingly to my right. I turned left. I looked away. I shopped. I left. I didn't look back. The car park was filled with people old to young and alcohol was everywhere I turned. In all corners of this tiny beachside microcosm there were the vague, illusory promises of alcohol blowing in the afternoon breeze. The thrill of the night that will never meet these lofty expectations hung in the evening air. The enticement of revelry that will always fall catastrophically short of what we all chased.

I left. I collected my daughter and headed to the beach for an evening swim. Teenagers lined the grassy dunes at the beach's entrance. Beers, smokes, music, the trappings of youth, the tranquil air alive with pulsating life of hormones and booze in the summer air. I turned away with my daughter, who ran into the water with a fervor that widened my smile more than anything else I could imagine. She splashed and played until the sun set in the serene summer sky. There is nothing I could buy in the liquor store that would make this better.

It was a long weekend here. It was a weekend that was always the monumental blowout of the year. It's one that I have historically played gigs, smashed drugs and drunk like there was no tomorrow.

But there is a tomorrow. There are people whose tomorrows are very much affected by our todays. I am so glad I was here to see the simple delight of a young girl howling like a wolf cub at the sunset over the southern seas of my home.

When I see how pervasive alcohol is, it makes me admire everyone that is struggling against it all the more. It's such a massive, difficult, and revolutionary act to turn our backs on such an omnipresent and socially permitted substance. It's addictive as anything, but it's also completely acceptable to drink in all facets of life. Until it isn't. Until we breach the slippery agreement of "moderate drinking" and do something outside the amorphous social contract and drink before our morning coffee, or drive hammered, or take drugs to get through the day of parenting because we're still wired and smashed from the night before, all of which I am guilty.

But things shift. Give it time. Let the dust settle. Not every day will be a battle. Things can get easier. They can get harder too. But not every trigger will always be a trigger. Patience. Perseverance. Commitment. It's these things that are rebellious, life changing and life saving. Every single one of us has unlimited potential to live those things. We just have to decide what we want and go for it. Sobriety is a struggle. But it's a worthwhile struggle, and one that I'm eternally grateful for.

ABOUT THE AUTHOR

Drew Charles is a reformed party animal musician turned author from Melbourne, Australia. He is committed to sharing his experience with alcohol and drugs to break the stigma of substance use and dependence. He has published a number of poems and short prose pieces and has appeared on podcasts for *One Year No Beer* and *Over the Influence*. Drew also has a PhD in literature and is an avid surfer, golfer, and baker of cookies.

Printed in the USA
CPSIA information can be obtained
at www.ICGtesting.com
JSHW022326140824
68134JS00019B/1325